FROM A ROTTEN APPLE TO A GEORGIA PEACH

By Toya McCray

From A Rotten Apple to A Georgia Peach

Copyright 2018 It's BOLD Publishing

Published by It's BOLD Publishing
Desoto Texas 75115

13-ISBN: 978-0-9987736-3-6 (paperback)

All rights reserved.

Without limiting the rights under copyright reserved above, no part of this publication may be reproduced, stored in or introduced into a retrieval system, or transmitted, in any form, or by any means (electronic, mechanical, photocopying, recording, or otherwise), without the prior written permission of both the copyright owner and the above publisher of this book.

If you purchased this book without the cover you should be aware that this book is stolen property. It was reported as "unsold and destroyed" to the publisher and neither the author nor the publisher has received any payment for this "stripped book".

Printed in the United States of America.

ACKNOWLEDGEMENTS

I am grateful for my friends and family. I will never be ashamed of anything that I went through to get where I am today. I am truly blessed to have the opportunity to share my life experiences with you.

Special thanks to my childhood friend, Jeannine for all of her help and patience. Shout out to all my friends and family, both fictional and nonfictional. Special thanks to Tasia Williams for typing everything for me. Thanks to my sister and brother for helping me with some of my memories from the past and all those who listened and gave me the courage to put my thoughts on paper.

Last but not least, I thank you, THE READER. Thank you again for reading my book. If you've never been to Brooklyn, New York or Atlanta Georgia, please visit. This book is dedicated to one of my best friends Sj24 *aka* Sequana Cooke Harris who left us too soon on August 14, 2017. I remember talking to her about the book and she suggested I change the title. Rest in Peace my best friend forever.

God Bless, and thanks again!

Table of Contents

Chapter 1: The Early Years Bedford Stuyvesant, Brooklyn, New York (Bed-Stuy Do or Die) 1

Chapter 2: "Coney Island" 13

Chapter 3: Back to Bed-Stuy 23

Chapter 4: C.I.-Sheepshead Bay, Brooklyn - & No Bat! 43

Chapter 5: On My Own 57

Chapter 6: Momma's Baby 71

Chapter 7: Tough Good Byes 87

Chapter 8: Welcome to Atlanta, GA! 113

EPILOGUE

Chapter 1

The Early Years Bedford Stuyvesant, Brooklyn, New York (Bed-Stuy Do or Die)

I remember growing up in Bed Stuy, Brooklyn, NY, Summer Projects to be exact. 4 Lewis Avenue was my home and I lived on the top floor in apartment 6-C.

"Y'all might as well start walking," a teenage boy coming out of the staircase said. You could tell he was used to this.

"The elevator broke." He quipped and walked right passed us.

"Ah-man." My sister Aliceia let her shoulders collapse and dropped her bottom lip in frustration. She dragged her shoes against the gray, speckled floor and headed towards the stair case. Her tall frame moved closer to the door and I stood still.

"I don't wanna walk." I said with tears forming in my eyes.

Aliceia kept walking toward the staircase and said, "Well, what you plan on doing cause I ain't carrying you!"

I sucked my teeth and headed to the staircase. For some reason, it always smelled like urine. We often had to jump over puddles of piss to get to the next floor, and don't be surprised if you got to my floor and there was someone getting high or having sex.

The projects were crazy like that. Other times you could catch some kids puffing on a cigarette they stole from their parents.

We finally made it to the 6th floor, huffing and puffing like oversized people trapped in our tiny bodies. I had to exaggerate my huffs and puffs and the more I did, the more Aliceia did too.

After eating a light snack and drinking a nice cold cup of lemonade, I asked,

"Aliceia, can I go outside?"

"Not until you finish your homework."

"I ain't got no homework—it's Friday."

"Well sit down for a minute and let me catch my breath and you know you can't wear your school clothes outside, so go change."

I ran to our room and started looking for a pair of jeans and a matching shirt. Running down the steps was a lot better than walking up. There wasn't not one huff or puff from me or Aliceia.

I saw some guys with a soda can near the fire hydrant (we called it a Johnny Pump). They started scratching the can by rubbing it back and forth on the concrete. The friction allowed the ends to pop off. Then another guy got a monkey wrench and turned the top and the opening, allowing the water to flow out. They placed the now hollow can over the water giving anyone the advantage of controlling the stream of water. We all ran out in the street to get wet, watching very closely for cars passing by.

"Y'all better not wet my car." An older man yelled while driving a nice, shiny, Cadillac.

The guy put the can down for a second and as soon as he hit the gas they showered the car with a full stream of water. My face lit up with a smile.

CHAPTER 1

"Y'all stupid little bastards—I said don't wet my fucking car!"

His ranting and raving was muffled because he had all his windows up but we could tell he was mad as hell.

We all got side tracked when the sound of a Mr. Softee ice cream truck rang in the air.

"Mommy, mommy, I need money for the ice cream truck." That was the gang of us in chorus whenever that truck rolled through our neighborhood.

"I don't see no damn ice cream truck," someone's mother would yell out the window.

"We can hear it, it's coming!"

Children would start gathering underneath the windows waiting for their parents to wrap the money in a piece of tissue or aluminum foil to throw it out the window.

On this particular day, I had some change in my pocket and gave it to the man perched outside the truck, standing on my tippy toes. I sat on the side of the curb allowing the water to run in between my toes as I ate my Bomb Pop.

"Give me some of the Icee." My dad's deep voice said.

"Daddy, Daddy!!" I cried leaping from the curb to get in his arms.

"Girl, get off me you're wet."

"So, it's hot outside. You'll dry fast. Wanna get wet with me?"

"No baby," —-Daddy tired."

"Okay. You're about to be real tired 'cause the elevator broke!" With an evil grin, I turned and walked ahead of my father.

"Got dammit, ain't this a bitch." He swore as he walked toward the building. He lingered outside for a few minutes and talked to the neighbors before hiking up six flights of steps after a long day of work. A lot of the older kids started picking each other up and carrying them deep into the stream of water. That was my queue to take a seat. I waved to Mrs. Rose, who was always looking out of her front window.

"Hey baby, how was school today?"

"Good."

"Where your daddy at?"

"He just went upstairs."

"Oh, okay."

"You got some candy Mrs. Rose?"

"Sure, and I made a cake too!!"

"Can I have some?"

"Of course, you can."

Looked over at Aliceia.

"Aliceia, can I go get some cake from Mrs. Rose?"

"How you know Mrs. Rose got cake?"

"Because, she told me."

"What I told you about asking people for stuff?"

"I didn't ask for cake. I asked for a piece of candy and she told me she had cake."

"Just come on Toya. You get on my nerves."

"Fine, then don't ask me for none of my cake."

We ran upstairs and Mrs. Rose was waiting for me with her door open.

"Ima call you from the window when she's done."

"Okay." My sister answered as she tried to hide her annoyance.

Mrs. Rose's house was always so nice and clean, but she had a few roaches here and there; my father said they didn't eat much. I was sitting in the window while she was cutting me a piece of cake.

"Go wash your hands, sweetie."

As I returned to the kitchen, we heard a lot of yelling and screaming coming from in front of the building. Mrs. Rose went to the

CHAPTER 1

window and I trailed right behind her.

"What the hell they yelling for?"

"Wow, look at that car?" I couldn't believe what I saw.

"Oh shit, who's that?"

We saw a cherry red convertible parked in the front of the building. *"Love and Happiness"* by Al Green was blasting from the car radio.

"Make you do wrong, make you do right..."

All the kids started running to the car and as I looked down, I saw a very pretty, white lady, sitting in the passenger's side with the cutest little, white puppy I had ever seen.

"*Aww, look at that little puppy.*" I cried out.

"Can I go back outside Mrs. Rose?"

"Sure baby, let me walk you to the door and let your sister know you're coming downstairs."

I dashed out of the front door, down the steps and wiggled my way through the crowd of kids.

"Can I hold your puppy?"

"Of course." The white woman replied as she began to pass me the puppy.

His fur was so white, soft and he smelled good. I held him up and looked deep in his eyes. For a second, I wished that the puppy was mine. The woman must have had a sixth sense because she reached to take the puppy back. I glanced at her and noticed her fur coat slightly opened and I could see that she did not have anything on underneath the coat. With the rest of the kids in tow, I ran back to sit on the stoop and I saw Mr. Brown looking up and arguing with his wife, Ms. Nora.

"JUST THROW ME MY MUTHERFUCKING JACKET." Mr. Brown yelled angrily.

"I ain't giving you shit, you got some nerve," —-Ms. Nora placed her hand on her hip, "bringing another bitch around here!"

"Don't start Nora. You said get out, so I'm out!"

"Drop my jacket now because I ain't got the time for your bullshit!"

"Alright." Ms. Nora disappeared for a few minutes, then quickly returning to the window.

"Y'all kids move back!"

"Leave the damn kids alone— you see they're playing"

"Alrighttt, you asked for it!" Ms. Nora's arms peered through the bars on the window holding a black bag. Ms. Nora shifted the bag and then began to pour. Mr. Brown was holding his hands out so he could catch the bag not realizing it was liquid.

"OH MY GOD!" He yelled as the liquid splattered onto his hands, chest and face.

"Y'ALL KIDS COME IN THE BULDING." Someone yelled from the doorway.

Mr. Brown was yelling, screaming and holding his hands on his face. His face was melting like a piece of cheese that spills out in a frying pan when you're making a grilled cheese sandwich.

"TALK SHIT NOW, NIGGA!" Ms. Nora yelled as she continued to empty the bag.

Ms. Nora, like most people in our neighborhood, kept a concoction under the kitchen sink with lye (Drano), urine (piss) and honey, shaken up in a container. Rumor has it that the lye would burn your skin, the urine would keep it unclean (more chances of infection) and the honey would make it stick like glue.

Sirens rang out down the block; the cops and an ambulance arrived to take Mr. Brown to the hospital. By this time Ms. Nora was downstairs comforting her man. She jumped in the back of the van to stick by her husband.

CHAPTER 1

❦

Saturday mornings were the best. "A B C is easy as One, two, three. . ." we sang along with the Jackson 5 while watching their cartoon and eating a bowl of Captain Crunch or Lucky Charms.

Knock, knock, knock

"Who is it?"

"DON'T YOU OPEN THAT DOOR!" My father yelled.

"I'm not. I just wanted to see who it is."

"Go sit your nosey ass down and get that bowl off my couch."

"Yes, Daddy."

Aunt Jessie, who lived on the 5th floor had just come by our apartment.

"Hey George."

"Hey, how you doin'?"

"I wanted to know if Toya wanted to go with me to the supermarket."

"Yeah, I wanna go." I said quickly, my eyes as big as quarters.

"What the hell you doing ear hustling? I thought you were watching cartoons."

"I was until I heard my name." I grinned happily because I wanted so bad to be anywhere but at home.

"Go get your sweater. You know you get cold in the meat department!"

"Oh yeah, cause last time I had chill bumps, right, Aunt Jessie?"

"Yes, you did."

I ran to my room, grabbed a jacket, and hurried back to Aunt Jessie who stood by the door, dangling her keys. I couldn't wait to get outside and go into the big grocery store that had aisles and aisle of junk food that if I was well behaved, would become a treat!

Aunt Jessie always put me inside of the shopping cart, and I always got to hold any treat that was especially mines. We picked up collard greens, three boxes of macaroni, sharp and cheddar cheese, cake mix, eggs, frosting, corn meal, butter and a bag of puffed cheese doodles for myself. We got back to the house and she let me help her peel the leaves off the stems of the collard greens. I was so little that I had to stand in a chair while Aunt Jessie stood next to me in front of the other part of the sink.

"Who is that standing in my good chair?"

"Me, Toya!"

"What you doing?" That was uncle T.F. He was my favorite uncle because he would always treat me to something special whenever I saw him.

"Getting ready to help Aunt Jessie."

"You can't cook."

"Shiiit, yes I can."

"Watch your mouth little girl."

"Sorry."

"Oh, leave her alone Jessie. Guess what I got Toya?"

"Aunt Jessie brought me puffed cheese doodles." I interrupted.

"I got something better."

"What?"

He left out of the kitchen and returned with a huge teddy bear bigger than me. I hugged the teddy bear, jumping down out of the chair.

"Be careful girl before you hurt yourself."

"I love it, Uncle T.F. Thank you!"

He rubbed the top of my head.

"Remember we went to Graham Avenue last week and you stopped in front of the window and said how much you loved that teddy bear?"

CHAPTER 1

"Um-hum."

"Well now it's yours."

"I can take it home?"

"Yes."

Giving him lots of hugs and kisses, he smiled. When I went home later that evening, I placed my new stuffed animal on top of my leopard toy chest. I was the happiest little girl in the world.

Weekends at my house were usually filled with close friends and family, playing cards, listening to music and drinking. My mother would come over and cook fried chicken, fish (whities and porgies only), macaroni and potato salad, just to name a few things. There was always an empty mayonnaise jar from the house. Every time people put bets up, the house got a cut.

"SOMEBODY DIDN'T PUT UP!" Ms. Pearl, raised her voice while still shuffling the cards.

"I got it. Damn Pearl. You ain't give me a chance."

"Well hurry up Angie, so I can take all your money."

"You a lie, I'm gonna send you home broke like I did last week."

"BOTH Y'ALL HEFFAS SHUT UP!" My father shouted. "'CAUSE I PAY THE COST TO BE THE BOSS IN THIS HOUSE!"

"George, watch your mouth."

"You shut the hell up too, Harriet."

Harriet was my mother. She had been married to my father for some time. They mostly got along until they didn't.

"That's why Toya talk the way she does. Always cussing."

"Well she don't curse at me, so that's all that matters." My father stood there proudly with his chest popped out. I smirked at his arrogance. He had no idea the cuss words running through my thoughts.

"Hey Toya, you winning all the money?" Ms. Barbara, one of our nosey neighbors, asked with a huge grin on her face. — "Let me borrow something."

"Motherfucker you know I ain't got no damn job and neither do yo' ass. How the hell you gonna pay me back? Shit." The worlds just rolled off my tongue like an old pro. My mother shifted her feet and looked at me pointedly.

"Alright now Toya, in the room—NOW." Everybody burst out laughing.

While the adults played black jack, pity pat, poker and tank, the kids were all in the room playing cards as well. We only played for nickels and dimes but you could easily make $5.00 to $10.00 if it was allowance week. We used to take turns running to the store for adults, which also gave you the chance to make money because they always gave you the change.

One night my brother wasn't home and my sister couldn't find her key. We were looking for my parents who were playing cards at a friend's house and we were ready to go home.

"Yo hurry up. Put that shit on, listen, we got ten minutes. In and out." That was the conversation between a few guys in the hallway as we were about to head to their friend's apartment. It was the same apartment that the guys were huddled in front of.

"Alright let's do this, you got the pistol just in case?"

"Just knock on the fucking door."

We could hear a lot of voices and music playing, but nobody came to the door as they knocked. Two more knocks and we started to hear footsteps. We froze in our tracks.

"Everybody ready?" One of the guys asked.

They pushed the lady down who opened the door.

"Y'all know what it is." He said as one of the guys held the door open. A smaller guy with no teeth pushed thru and passed around a dingy pillowcase.

CHAPTER 1

We walked closer and looked inside like we were watching a movie.

"Put all y'all shit inside quickly. Wallets, jewelry and all the money on the table. Pockets inside out. Let's go! Check their socks and those bitches' titties. You know they hide their little change purses in there!"

"Everybody do as they're told and nobody gets hurt."

"Got dammit! They got us."

"Check that nigga twice and shut the fuck up before I bust a cap in your ass!"

"You talk a lot of shit with that gun in your hand. Put that shit down and I'll tear you a new ass hole!"

"You don't want none old man. You better shut the fuck up before your wife be shopping for a new black dress."

"Shut up George and just do what they say before you get all of us killed." Mr. Pete uttered thru his clenched teeth. Within a matter of minutes, the guys had a bag full of items and money and hauled ass out the door and down the stairs. Aliceia and I stood in a daze as the adults cussed and argued with one another about whose fault it was that the robbery took place.

Monday mornings were difficult. After a weekend of company, we had to get up early in the morning to go to school and my dad had work. My poor sister had to get up extra early because she had to get me ready as well. She had to do our hair, make sure our homework was completed, take out something for dinner and pray that my brother came in from selling the morning paper and hot rolls with butter before we left. It was always a little nerve-wracking wondering if he got caught by the police or worst.

He used to steal the paper and rolls and deliver them before the real delivery person got there. Sometimes if he had a good morning he would give my sister $3.00. If it was a bad day she would get $1.00. He always shared no matter how much it was because we were taught to look out for one another. And if one of us had a fight, we all had a fight.

Every morning most of the kids would meet in front of our building and walk to school together. It was safer in groups because you never knew what you might see along the way. Our father taught us not to talk to strangers or some of the adults he spoke to when he wasn't around.

"Just 'cause I speak to someone doesn't mean he's my friend."

Chapter 2

"Coney Island"

"Now I lay me down to sleep, I pray the Lord my soul to keep. If I die before I wake, I pray the Lord my soul to take. I pray for my friends and my family, especially my mommy and daddy that they get back together, Amen."

I said this prayer over and over hoping that my parents would get back together.

"So, daddy, you spoke to mommy? Is she ready to come home?"

"I don't know. Ask your mother."

I went in the kitchen, climbed on the chair and dialed the number posted on the wall. On the third ring, she picked up.

"Ma?"

"Hey baby, how you doing?"

"Fine!! Daddy said ask you if you were ready to come home?"

"I'm not about to talk about that fool! How's your sister and brother?"

"They good."

"Well— I'll see y'all this weekend." There was a long pause. It felt awkward. I could tell this wasn't easy for my mother. I knew deep down inside she missed us.

"What you want mommy to cook for dinner?"

"I don't know. We'll think of something."

"Mommy loves you."

"I love you too, bye." I held the phone in my hand and listened as it clicked a few times then hung it up. I stared at the rotary and counted backwards the numbers trying to fight back the tears. I wanted us to be a family in the same house. I hopped of the chair and went into my room. I distracted myself and started thinking of ways to get on my sisters last nerves.

My father was working nights at the time so we were what you called latched key kids. We would tie our own key around our neck using an old shoe string. We weren't allowed to let anyone in the house except our cousins, the Adams Family. They lived on the fifth floor. There were seven of them and two other cousins who we spent a lot of time with. We also spent a lot of time with my cousin Linda, who lived up the block on 22 Lewis.

"Go get the grease so I can do your hair. You wanna come with me up to my school?"

"Yeah."

I ran and got the stuff off the dresser. My cousin Linda braided my hair up into a ponytail. If she was busy, Tracy would do it. My other cousin, Sharon, always gave me a nicely picked afro or ponytails. I loved spending the night at their house. It was always an adventure. One night it was storming pretty bad and the lights started to flicker.

"You know what that means Toya?" Uncle T.F asked with a sinister look on his face.

CHAPTER 2

"No, what?"

"It means somebody's gonna, die tonight."

"No, it does not." I rolled my eyes, but deep down inside, I was scared.

"Yes, it does. Y'all turn that T.V. off and all the lights. Everybody come sit on the floor in the living room and stay away from the windows."

Uncle T.F. told us a story about a guy who was coming out from the store in a bad storm and got electrocuted. He was found dead underneath a big tree. By now, I was beyond being a little scared, and I wanted to go to bed. When we went in the bedroom, there were wings on the posts of the beds giving the illusion of a person's head. I started crying and my Aunt Jessie let me get in the bed with her until I fell asleep. I'm still afraid of going out when it's thundering and lightning. I swear it should have been a crime for adults to traumatize kids with spooky stories.

Sometimes on the weekends, we would also go to my aunt Joanne's house, who lived on Green Avenue. This was another part of Bedford Stuyvesant that had a different vibe from the Projects or Lewis Avenue. On Greene Avenue, they were always cooking out, listening to music and playing cards, just like we did but without the restrictions of living so close to one another. There was space, direct access to the streets, corner stores, and eclectic venues within reach.

My cousins had a drum set and I used to love to watch them play. That was a time when we were all together and I was able to fit in. Being that I was the youngest, when the older kids rode their bikes or played games in the street, I had to sit on the stoop. Even though I was stuck on the stoop with a poked-out lip and watching everybody enjoy riding their bikes, doing popped wheelies, riding on handle bars, peddling backwards as they leaned in, and making smooth turns only to ride past me and do it again and again, I could watch them play for days as long as we were all together.

One time the older kids were riding up and down the block and I noticed my cousin Sharon coming down the block with my sister on the back of the bike. All of a sudden, I heard a lot of yelling, I looked down the block and I saw a crowd forming. My cousin ran past me into the house and everybody started barreling out of the house like a herd of elephants. With no one left in the house, my mother picked me up and started running down the block. There was such a big crowd, you couldn't tell who it was.

"Move back, who is it?"

"Oh my God. No Lord! Please!!"

All you could see was a pair of sneakers peeking from underneath a white sheet. My mother handed me to my Aunt Joanne and bent down to pull back the sheet. My sister's bright eyes lit up as my mother grabbed her and hugged her.

"You had me scared to death. Why did you pull the sheet up?"

"Because everybody was staring at me and I was scared. I'm sorry ma." Aliceia answered.

"Are you okay? Can you walk?"

"I think so." My sister said as she struggled a little to get up. We all walked back up the block and that the first time I noticed that my family was close. If one fell, it was like all of us fell.

Thank God my sister was ok. I don't know what I would've done without her. A couple of weeks later she was back on the bike like nothing happened. Eventually, I learned to ride too. I wasn't the best at it because I was nervous.

When they rode around the buildings, circling four streets, they told me that I couldn't go because I rode too slow, so I sat on the stoop with my Aunt Jessie, again watching and waiting, but soon enough I was able to join in on some of the fun.

"Hey Toya, what's wrong, why you looking so sad?" My cousin Don Q asked.

"Sharon and Aliceia said I can't ride with them because I ride too slow."

"Well maybe if you take those training wheels off you can go faster."

"But I can't ride without the training wheels!" I exclaimed looking at him square in the eye.

"Who said you can't?"

The real reason was that I was terrified. I needed my training wheels even if they made me go too slow.

"I'm gonna fall."

"So, get back up and try again."

"I'm too little."

"No, you're not. I taught Sharon and Aliceia how to ride when they were your age. You five, right?"

"Yup." That was my response whenever someone said, *"You're five, right?"*

"Okay, then let's go. Get your bike."

By this time Aliceia was headed up the block. I stood there and got on my tippy toes and watched her as she got closer to me. I was so excited I couldn't wait to ask her for the key.

"Aliceia, I need the key."

"For what," She asked as she squeezed the brakes and stopped in front of me and Don Q.

"Don gonna teach me how to ride without my training wheels."

Aliceia smiled, showing her teeth. She pulled the silver key chain from around her neck and handed it to my cousin. We headed upstairs quickly.

We went back downstairs and I grabbed my bike as quickly as I could. Don Q could tell I was excited and he just let me do all that a five-year-old could do and assisted only when necessary.

With my bike beside me, I pushed it as we walked to the basketball court.

When we arrived, my cousin told me to put my feet on the pedals, and hold on tight to the handlebars and push the pedals down like I did on my big wheel. The bike started to wiggle unsteadily and I fell. I felt like crying and started to just cry and give up.

"Get up, don't cry. You can do it."

This time he held on the seat with one hand and helped me steer the handlebars with the other. As I peddled, he walked with me for a few feet then let go and I fell again, my knee was bleeding. He wiped it off and told me, "Come on let's do it again." I repeated this several times until I was riding without him holding me. I returned home with a bruise on my right knee, but I could ride with the older kids. I couldn't wait to tell my mother and father.

Soon, friends and family members started getting shot, bit by dogs really bad, robbed and raped. Rumors were spreading that there was a rapist on the loose in the projects and people started making plans to move. My brother Glen started getting into trouble too, fighting a lot, cutting school and involving himself with the wrong crowd. The absence of my mother wasn't helping the situation either, so my father decided to relocate to Coney Island, Brooklyn, New York.

We spent the night over my godparents Loretta and Ronnie's house and in the morning, we drove to our new place.

"Do I have my own room?"

"No, Toya, you will share a room with your sister"

"What about my friends?"

"You can still see your friends on the weekends."

"Can we still visit 4 Lewis?"

"Yes, Toya."

"Are other people moving to Coney Island too?"

"No, Toya."

"Is mommy coming?"

"I don't know."

"Can I get a cat or a dog?"

"We'll see."

"How far is my new school?"

"Across the street."

"Did you tell my teacher I wasn't coming back?"

"Yes."

"Did you pack my toy chest and my teddy bears? Is my rabbit coat I got from Aunt Loretta in the closet?"

"Alright Toya with all the darn questions."

"Okay, one more, what floor are we on?"

"Twelve. Now shut up!"

"What about when the elevators break down, I'm not walking up 12 flights of stairs."

"Well they have two elevators and a front and back staircase."

"What, oh my God. It must be real big."

"You'll see, and we have a terrace."

"I ain't going out on no terrace 12 stairs up. What if I fall?"

"You can't fall dummy. They have metal bars all around it."

Once we parked the car and walked to the building, my father pointed up to our apartment. It was so high up, it looked like it was in the sky. There was a basketball court/handball court on the side of the building, a playground in the back of the building, and benches with tables in the middle on the other side. I felt like the Jefferson's, and we were moving on up. We took the elevator to the 12th floor, and then made a left through the swinging doors to the last apartment on the right side. The floors were clean, walls were graffiti free and it smelled like cherries. The apartment was much bigger than our last place and my father had his own personal bathroom inside his room. I was in love with this place. I immediately went to the terrace and looked down. There was a big park across the street. I saw a large beach and a big metal thing that looked like a parachute. I saw a lot of other projects and tall buildings. Some pink, brown, and white. Ours was brown, black and orange. My sister and I chose the second bedroom because there was another bathroom in front of our room. I looked out the window and saw a big bridge. We went in the kitchen and checked out the cabinets, refrigerator and I noticed we didn't have any food.

"Daddy, you know we ain't got no food?"

"Yeah fool, the apartment doesn't come with food girl. When y'all get settled we're gonna go to Key Food or Pathmark."

We went to the supermarket and it was packed. I noticed a pizza shop and I asked my dad if we could get a slice and an Italian ice. They had games in the back as well.

After we got home, I went in my room I shared with my sister and played with my imaginary friend, Nancy, while my sister helped my dad with the groceries. Nancy and I played house with my dolls and I asked her if she was hungry. I shared the last of my pizza with her. I saw some kids outside and asked my sister if we could go outside too; she said tomorrow. The next day we went outside and I immediately started making friends. We made plans to play again the next day.

In the morning, I went downstairs to the laundromat with my dad to help wash clothes. In our other building, you had to walk. While the clothes were washing, my dad and I sat outside on the side of the building.

CHAPTER 2

"Oh, look daddy, we can play checkers."
"You can't beat me in no checkers."
"Yes, I can, all we need is some pieces."
"Well I don't see no checker pieces."
"We can use rocks and sticks."
"Okay. You can find them while I smoke my cigarette."

He beat me of course, but it was a good game to help time pass. Growing up we didn't always have much but it was the little things that counted. We would create a game, teach others how to play and enjoy ourselves.

On Fridays, when we got our allowance, my sister took me to the candy store. I bought pretzels, jelly cookies, squirrel nuts, orange slices, cherry balls, big boi's, tootsie rolls and now and laters.

"You keep eating all that candy, and you ain't gon' have no teeth when you get older." Well I guess we both weren't going to have any teeth because Aliceia ate as much candy as I did.

"Well I'll worry about that then."
"Alright hard headed, don't come crying to me when you get a toothache."

Summer was almost over and we prepared to go shopping for new clothes and school supplies. I called my mother and she brought me more clothes.

"I like your new room." She smiled. Did you make any friends?"
"Yeah."
"That's nice sweetie. I told you it would be okay."
"Where's your new school?"
"Across the street."
"Oh, wow! That's great! Are you scared?"
"A little, but I met some kids in the building that go there. Sherri, Vanessa, and Kevin."

"Oh, okay, well if you need me just call me."

I got a little sad as she started to leave. As much as I loved going to the big park because they had swings, monkey bars, a see-saw, sliding boards and steps that we played on— they also had a small pier where you could go fishing, I loved having my mother around more. I missed her.

"Make sure you stick the hook all the way through the worm so it doesn't come off."

"Okay daddy, I got it."

Chapter 3

Back to Bed-Stuy

Transitioning from a little girl to a teenager can be very difficult. You're not a child anymore, yet and still, you're not an adult either. From public school to junior high school, there can be a lot of peer pressure and a need to fit in as well as having an identity crisis.

My father, brother, sister and I all had new friends. My mother decided to give their marriage one last chance but things didn't work out, so we went back to spending time with her on the weekends. Glen started getting into trouble again.

"I'm tired of going through this shit with you, Glen. You are the man of the house when I'm not home. The next time your ass gets locked up, I'm gonna let you rot in jail. Now you got two choices: either you go to college or go to the army."

There was no way Glen was going to stay out of trouble. The time for him to decide on making better choices came sooner rather than later. He went to the recruiting station on his own. My brother had an open case, so they offered him a deal. His recruiter told him if he enlisted in the army that he could get his charges dropped.

"So, you telling me if I go to the army I don't have to go to jail?" Glen asked.

"That's what I'm telling you."

"Bet, that's a deal."

He completed the paperwork on Monday and was surprised when they told him that he had to leave Wednesday. We were all crying. It was very sad to see my brother go away for four years, but I would have rather seen him in the army, fighting for our country versus in jail. He promised to write and send me gifts, which he did every chance he got. As the years went by, he started to get bigger. He had muscles on top of muscles. I couldn't wait for him to come home so I could tell him who had been messing with me so he could beat them up. Especially since he had been boxing. I would've told my father but with his temper, he'd be the one in jail.

It was a regular day at school and we heard the bells ringing, letting us know it was a routine fire drill. All the kids in the class quickly walked to the front door, down the hall and took the steps to the first landing. You had to be very quiet during a fire drill so you could hear the instructions in case of a real fire.

"What we having for lunch?" My friend Gretchen asked, as she looked around.

"I don't know." I responded quickly.

"You stepping on the back of my shoe." Another friend, Ada, said in her deep West Indian accent.

"Shh. Be quiet." I hissed.

"OUT OF LINE NOW!" Mr. Lipton yelled as he grabbed me by my tiny elbow. Mr. Lipton was built like a giant cyclops but with two eyes. He rarely smiled and was what most would call, *the enforcer.*

CHAPTER 3

One look and kids thought twice about acting out of line.

"I wasn't talking. I was telling them to be quiet."

"You're always talking Toya. That's all you do is talk, talk, talk."

"But I wasn't talking."

"Shut up." He said and pushed me against the wall. I froze for half of a second. Then I took off in the opposite direction. Running.

"Oh my God. Where are you going?"

Running as fast as I could I darted out of the lunchroom to the emergency exit, setting off the fire alarm. I ran all the way home and called my father. Without breathing, I attempted to tell my story as snot and tears covered my face.

"Calm down Toya. I can't understand you."

"My teacher pushed me because he thought I was talking during a fire drill." I was finally able to say.

"Okay just stay in the house until your sister gets home. We'll go up to the school tomorrow. Are you okay? Did he hurt you?"

"He just hurt my arm."

"Okay, I'll see you when I get home. I love you."

"I love you too daddy."

That night my father checked my bruises, questioned me like there was no end in sight, and tucked me in with a kiss.

The next day my father brought me to school and waited for my teacher to arrive to the classroom. We walked in silence as other students watched. Their tiny heads, and shrill voices, watched and waited for what was next. My father stood by the door and I stood right beside him.

Mr. Lipton walked in and didn't see us and headed towards his desk. The classroom that had only a few students, fell into a deep silence, which wasn't unusual because we all feared Mr. Lipton. But this silence was different. One by one, those tiny heads began to sink onto their desks as some friends and a few classmates watched and waited for Mr. Lipton to get his comeuppance.

"You Mr. Lipton?" My father asked curtly.

"Yes sir, I am. And you are?" Mr. Lipton replied quizzically. You could tell he was caught off guard.

"Mr. George McCray. Toya McCray's father."

"Yes, about yesterday. I didn't mean to grab her like that. I wanted to apologize but she ran out the building so fast." Mr. Lipton tried to explain.

It was about to be a tennis match because each time one the adults spoke, tiny heads shifted to that person's statements.

"Well, whether she was talking or not, don't you ever put your hands on my child again. Do you understand?"

"Yeah, well I was trying too..."

"Don't try next time. Don't touch my child or you'll see this gun."

My father pulled his gun from behind his back, cocked it and emptied one shiny gold bullet from its chamber. Gasps filled the room.

"The next time it's going up your ass." Not one chuckle was heard. Not even from me.

I was so scared. I thought my father was going to shoot him. My father looked at me and winked and I just smiled. My father's temper could sometimes be a lot to deal with.

"Go sit down."

I scurried to my seat next to Ada and tried to pretend that my father wasn't about to set it off in my third-grade classroom. When the rest of the class joined us, we all sat like darling angels with sinister grins, daring Mr. Lipton to try one of us again. He never did.

CHAPTER 3

My father made several attempts to get my mother back. It was obvious that my mother wasn't coming back, so my father started dating. He told us about a lady he met, named Avis who lived in the Bronx.

"Do she have any kids?" I asked.

"Yeah she has a son a few years younger than you Toya."

So, we got in my father's car and drove all the way to the Bronx. She had a nice two-bedroom apartment. Her son was very sweet.

"I'm hungry daddy." I growled at him because he was in another zone with Avis.

"Me and Avis gonna go to the store we'll be right back." He smiled at us as they hurried out the door.

It seemed like they took forever to return.

"I'm hungry Aliceia,"

"Well, you have to wait until daddy comes back."

"Yeah you have to wait till my mom comes back."

"Shut up little boy. I know y'all got something here to eat."

I went to open the refrigerator door and my sister slammed it before I could get a glimpse.

"I said, wait. You can't go to people's house and touch their stuff without permission Toya. I'm telling daddy."

"MOOOOOVE. SHE ABOUT TO GET US SOMETHING ANYWAY." I yelled.

"NO, MAKE ME!" Aliceia shouted back.

Aliceia pushed me down and when I got up I went to the cabinet and got a bag of flour and started throwing flour on her. She opened the refrigerator and got the ketchup and squirted some on me. I went back to the cabinet to get some grits and syrup. She got mustard and mayonnaise and before we knew it, we were laughing and covered in food.

"Oh my God, what happened?" Avis asked as she looked around at her kitchen covered in condiments.

"She started it." Aliceia said pointing to me

"No, she started it." I said as I pointed back at her.

"Are you gonna tell our father?"

"Not if you hurry up and clean up." Avis said as she disappeared out of the kitchen.

That was the last time we saw Avis.

Then there was a lady named Barbara. I couldn't stand her for some reason. I made up a song about her called, "No Hair, No Teeth, Barbara." Next was Juanita, a pretty, light skinned woman who dressed nice. She had around four or five kids. Our families were close growing up together. She lived in Marcy Projects, which wasn't far from Sumner Projects. One of her sons, Alfred, started getting into trouble, not going to school, stealing, robbing people and staying out past curfew so my dad decided to take him in for a while since we moved to Coney Island. And I loved when my cousin Sharon would visit because she was working in Coney Island and we used to gang up on Alfred all the time.

"You need to stop being so mean and read your holy Qur'an, and eating pork is going to kill all y'all one day." Alfred would tell us.

"Shut the fuck up! We were all raised on pork and ain't nobody died."

"Why do you think the pig can't lift his head?"

"Because that's how pigs are born."

"No, it's because it's the only animal punished by God. It's also the only animal that eats its own urine, feces and garbage, but you

CHAPTER 3

continue to put that mess in your stomach. You might as well eat out the dumpster full of trash."

"No, that's where you should eat and get out my house. My father cooks pork all the time. Have you had this conversation with him? What do the Qur'an say about stealing? Is that okay? You're a thief."

"So, riddle me this, if God's name is Allah, then why do people scream oh my God?"

"Allah is God, Toya."

"Alright Alfred, I›m tired of arguing with you. *Oops,* I mean Born."

Born was Alfred's nickname. It was part of his new identity as a Muslim in the Nation of Islam. He had strong beliefs about Allah, not eating pork, and not trusting the white man. But stealing, he never had beliefs about that.

He continued to bring stolen merchandise in the house then would lie to my father about it. One day he pissed me off so bad, I waited until he fell asleep on the couch and I put rubbing alcohol on the couch, sprinkled a little on him, lit a match and ran out the house. A couple of days later he was gone. Thank God I didn't burn the house down. But at least Alfred left and never came back.

Juanita's other son Dehaven was my heart. He took me everywhere and treated me like his little sister. He loved rapping and he and his friend Sean were pretty good. One day Dehaven got into some beef with the Grimes sons, Nuka and Billy, who lived on the 10th floor. We told Sean just in case they tried to jump Dehaven.

"Nah I don't wanna fight." Sean replied. His voice shook in fear.

"Well, we will jump in and help you." —-- "We ain't scared of them."

"And Sean, you need to keep your punk ass in Marcy because if one of us fight, we all fight."

"My father would kick your ass all up and down his house if I told him what you just said."

Sean looked at me for a second then agreed to help us if Dehaven needed us.

Every Sunday was like Thanksgiving at my house, cards, drinks and lots of food.

"Daddy?"

"What?"

"You need to start charging these niggas. Everybody comes to eat, drink, and nobody brings anything or tries to help clean up. I'm tired of this shit!"

"You need to watch your mouth, little girl."

"I'll clean up Toya." Linda said as she began moving about the kitchen.

"No, this ain't your house. Daddy needs to put his foot down because that's a lot of money being spent every Sunday. When we were in Bed-Stuy, they would take turns."

"Oh, hell no, and look at this shit here!"

"What, what." everybody turned around.

Tulup, one of my father's friends, had peed on the couch.

"Get your nasty ass out!" I said through clenched teeth.

I grabbed him by his arm to make him get up and get him out the door.

"You see daddy? This is ridiculous. So drunk, he can't even go to the bathroom."

"Alright Toya, you made your point." My father conceded.

CHAPTER 3

Tulup was so embarrassed. He didn't come back for over a month and the card games became fewer. Nobody wanted to deal with me, and people started leaving one by one.

"Never deny a person food, Toya."

"I'm not denying them, they can take their food and go home to their own house."

Another one of my father's friends, Brown Eyes, got on my nerves as well. Every time I turned around his wife had a black eye or swollen lip. She never came by when he was playing cards. Being I was a child, I couldn't say anything even though I knew something was wrong. One day we were sitting at the table and I could hear a lot of yelling, screaming, and the kids crying. I put a glass next to the wall so I could listen better. All of a sudden, I heard a bang and our clock fell off the wall and onto the floor.

Bang, bang, bang.

I banged on the wall. The walls continued to shake, so I knocked on their door. Brown Eyes, the woman beater, opened the door.

"Oh, hey Toya."

"Don't hey Toya me, you're making too much noise and y'all broke our clock."

"I'm sorry about that Toya."

"Well I'm telling my dad when he gets home."

"I'll come talk to him."

"And you better stop beating your wife or I'm calling the cops."

"She's okay we're not fighting."

"Then why she covering her face?"

"She's just tired."

"Um-hum, whatever! If I hear y'all acting a fool again, I'm calling 911. I'm trying to do my home……."

"Okay, Toya." Brown Eyes said as he quickly shut the door.

Brown eyes and Gloria lived across from each other. Gloria was a lot quieter. She was the one who introduced my dad to Linda. Linda was one of the last girlfriends that my dad ever dated. She was very pretty, had hazel eyes and a beautiful personality. Linda was the only one I learned to love like a mother. I don't know how she put up with my father sometimes.

"Hey Toya, how was school today?"

"Fine."

"I just want to let you know that I'm not trying to take your mother's place. I love your dad very much and I just hope that you would give me a chance. I heard about some of the things you did to some of his other girlfriends and I just want to let you know that I'm not going anywhere, so you won't be able to get rid of me that easy. "

"Well, we will see." I grinned and disappeared into my room.

It was time to get ready for my public-school graduation from PS. 329 in Coney Island. I told my mother all about Linda and thought they should meet.

"Ma, this Toya. I want daddy's girlfriend to come to my graduation but can you come over so you can meet her first?"

"Did you talk to your father?"

"Yeah and he said to talk to you."

"Okay, I'll come on Saturday."

"Thanks mommy, I love you."

"Love you too."

The meeting went well, but Linda said that she didn't want to disrespect my mother so she wouldn't be coming to my graduation. I was a little sad at first but I began to cry tears of joy when I saw Linda in the back of the auditorium.

My friends and I also traded pictures and promised to keep in touch. My closest friends at the time were Vanessa, Amanda, Felice,

Jeannine, Michelle (Caja), Lashawn, Darcell, Desha and one another girl named Gretchen, but everybody kind of distanced themselves from her because throughout the years she behaved like the class bully.

Most of us had been in the same class since the second-grade. You would think the bond we had would keep us close and looking out for one another, not hurting each other. Not sure what was going on in Gretchen's life at that time, but I always remember the name-calling, teasing, pulling hair and making us do things to degrade one another.

Fall was coming and it was time to start junior high school. I was happy to find out that Amanda, Felice and Lashawn would be there, as well as one of my neighbors, Selina and my boyfriend, Kevin.

Because rent started going up, my father was having a difficult time paying all of the bills. Linda didn't work and my mother helped us out as much as she could. We left our apartment and my father moved in with my uncle Jimmy down the block in 2980. We had to wait until my father found a more affordable place for us to live.

"Why can't I move in with you and Uncle Jimmy?" I asked.

"Because you don't need to be in the house with no grown man that's not your father!"

"He's family."

"I don't care, —the answer is NO!"

"So, can I move in with Glen and Laverne?"

"NO, because they don't have enough room—plus they have two small kids there already."

"Well, can I stay with Matt? I spend most of my time there anyway."

"Do you know how many people Matt got living there with her already? She doesn't want you there too."

"Well I'm going to ask her, if she says yes, can I stay?"

"Sure Toya, but I'd rather you go to your mothers."

Of course, Matt said yes. It was a total of 17 of us in the house. My Aunt Matt was not blood related, but she had a heart of gold and she had an open-door policy— she never locked her door. I had to travel almost 2 hours to school.

Our apartment wasn't ready so I commuted back-and-forth until the end of the school year. That summer we moved to 464 Hancock Street. I loved the long hallway and sitting on the stoop doing my stepmother Linda's hair. Everybody was sitting outside listening to music getting their hair braided, the kids jumping Double Dutch, or playing jacks on the stoop. My block was always busy. Cars constantly rolled up and down the street. It would get a little loud at times because there was a fire department on the corner. Neighbors acting a fool, fighting and arguing, so it was not a surprise to see a woman throwing her man's clothes out the window. It was always a show on my block and we stayed entertained.

I started intermediate school at Junior High School 35 in the fall. The school was ghetto.

"Alright, y'all hurry up and get to class, y'all got five minutes till the bell rings."

"Shut up bitch ain't nobody listening to you."

"Excuse me little girl you got something to say?"

"You better get out my face old lady"

"If I don't what you gon' do?" Our principal, Ms. Williams, asked.

Frances knocked the bullhorn away from her mouth. Principal

CHAPTER 3

Williams dropped the bullhorn to her side and started yelling at Frances, **"YOU BETTER WALK OFF BEFORE YOU REGRET IT LATER!"**

"You better walk before I pull that wig off!" Frances replied calmly.

"GIRL..." Ms. Williams shifted the weight of her body to one side as one foot tapped the floor. She looked at Frances sternly and Frances glared back at her.

Then Frances snatched Ms. Williams' wig off and they got to swinging. Ms. Williams grabbed Frances by her hair and Frances started punching and kicking her. The security guards came and broke it up. Two points for Frances. Zero for Ms. Williams.

Later in the week our math teacher, Ms. Stokes, was absent so the kids decided to show out. It was a little stuffy in the classroom, so they decided to open the windows.

"Aye yo. Where y'all going? To Nostrand?"

"You coming? Hurry up, take the back staircase near the gym."

"I'm telling, y'all cutting." Angela, my friend, said.

"Shut up." Ernest, the class shit starter, replied.

"You shut up before I hit you with the book."

"I dare you."

Carl, Ernest's friend, looked inside the desk and found several textbooks and threw the heavy textbooks out the window. Laughter erupted in the classroom.

"Damn, let's throw all these motherfuckers out. We can't do work with no books." A handful of the students gathered as many books as they could and started throwing them out the window.

"Y'all better watch those books." Someone yelled as they passed by.

It was nothing to see a parent come and beat their child in front of the class either.

"Everybody, listen up. We have a school trip to the Statue of Liberty in two weeks. Permission slips are due with the money. You can bring your own lunch and we will have lunches from the lunch room. I expect everyone to be on their best behavior."

The trip was fun and everyone behaved themselves going, but coming back a few kids had other plans.

"Can we stop at the store before we get on the train?"

"Yes, but y'all gotta hurry up. Y'all got 10 minutes."

"Okay, fine."

Inside the store the kids were using their *five finger discounts* stealing. I had saved up my allowance so me and my friend Angela were good. We got out the store and passed a huge fruit stand.

"BUM RUSH!" One of the students yelled.

Everybody started yelling, BUM RUSH and began taking and throwing fruit.

"GET AWAY FROM MY STORE!" Pakistani man yelled while swinging a long stick.

Everybody started running to the train station. Inside, my teacher was fuming, fumbling with the pass to show the clerk so she could open the gate for the unruly bunch.

"I know everybody was involved and y'all will not be able to go on any more trips this year and I will be making some phone calls."

"I ain't got no phone so I ain't worried." Headache said.

"Boy, I will go to your house if I have to because you were the ring leader."

CHAPTER 3

"No, I wasn't. I was at the store buying some potato chips and a quarter water."

We got to the next stop and we were just sitting there. Everybody emptied out their pockets, showing each other what they stole. A few kids got up and looked out the doors to see what was going on.

"Y'all sit down! Stop being so nosey!"

"Oh shit!" Corey said because he saw something as he squinted his eyes.

You could hear a lot of keys jingling as officers were running down the platform. Two of them stopped in our car and radioed for assistance.

"I need backup. I got 'em."

"What's going on officers?" Ms. Stokes asked confused.

"The owner of the fruit store reported that some of your kids were stealing. I'm gonna need for y'all to step off the train."

"They can't lock us up for some damn candy." Munchy said loudly.

"Close your mouth and get up." The officer said as he pointed to Munchy to stand.

"Let's go kids." Ms. Stokes demanded as we looked around in disbelief.

We got off the train and the cops collected all the candy from everybody.

"I paid for my stuff." I said to the officer as Ms. Stokes watched the officers grab pockets full of candy.

"Yeah she's good. I can't speak for the rest of them,".

I was so embarrassed. I couldn't wait to get home to tell my father about this one.

I had some good friends at this school, but Angela was my closest friend. She was a Jamaican girl that was raised by a single mother.

She was an only child and lived two houses down from me, but she wasn't allowed to hang outside on the block. Desiree was a big, pretty girl, also an only child, being raised by a single mother. Emma, and Munchy, had a sister who was also pretty, very Christian and was also raised by a single mother too. Desiree lived closer to the store. Munchy lived a few blocks down near my other friend Deloras. Deloras was raised by a single mother too and she had a sister. I remember this boy in my school named Curtis, who was always bothering me. Me and Angela used to jump him all the time, but he wouldn't stop. One day while we were walking home he decided to grab my book bag.

"You better give me my bag back."

"Or what? You can't catch me."

He ran and me and Angela chased him down. We got him on the floor and started punching and kicking him. He threw my book bag in the middle of the street and a car came and ran over it. I ran and picked it up.

"You gonna pay for my bag."

"I ain't paying for shit."

"Alright, we'll see."

We ran home and I saw my brother-in-law, Pop, sitting on the table.

"What's wrong? It looks like you been crying."

"Why were you runnin'?" Pop asked.

"This boy name Marcus keep bothering me in school and today he just threw my book bag in the street."

I showed him my bag.

"Where he at? He walking from school? How far he live?"

"Close to Gates Avenue." I replied.

"Okay, come on so we can catch him."

CHAPTER 3

Pop took off running.

"I can't go, Toya." Angela said.

"I know, Angela, I'll knock on your door and tell you what happened."

"Okay."

Me and Pop ran down Sumner Avenue and caught Marcus four blocks down.

"Aye-Yo. You, Marcus? Come here. And don't run because if I have to chase you I'm going to beat your ass." Marcus, was terrified. He didn't even see us coming. It was like magic, we were in his face.

"Why you keep fucking with my little sister?"

"I was just playing with her."

"No, you wasn't. You always bothering me."

Pop grabbed him by the collar of his shirt and lifted him up in the air. His shoes dangled and he tried to get free, which only pissed off Pop more.

"I think you owe her an apology."

"I'm sorry. — I'm sorry."

"Don't tell me, tell her." Pop said as he looked over at me. I was grinning.

"I' I' I'm sorry, Toya."

"And by Monday you better have her a new book bag or you're going to have to deal with me, again. You can get your brother, uncle or father . . ."

School was out and I had been seeing flyers all over the hood for a concert that was coming up at the Brooklyn Armory. My cousin,

Lisa, called me and asked me If I wanted to go. Of course, I said yeah. Since I did so well in school my father agreed to give me the money for the ticket and my mother bought me a new outfit. Performers included LL Cool J, Salt n Pepa, MC Shan and Marley Marl, MC Lyte, Biz Markie, and Big Daddy Kane.

The performers started to make their way to the stage. The place was packed. I thought my brother had some big speakers but these speakers were huge. Different color lights illuminated around the room. Everybody was singing along, enjoying themselves.

"Yo man, watch it you'll almost stepped on my foot." One guy said to this other guy next to him.

"Man move back you see it's crowded." Another one said.

"Yo, you tryin' to flex?"

"You don't want it."

And just like that, the guys started punching each other. The bouncers came and did their best to break up the fight. Then, around thirty minutes later—- **Pop, pop, pop**! Sounds like firecrackers going off rang out loud. Everybody started running. **Pop, pop, pop!** Three more shots were fired. My cousin grabbed my hand, but the crowd was so thick we got separated. People were crouching down along the street to find shelter because now, bullets were flying everywhere. You could smell the gunpowder in the air. I saw people crawling so I followed them and we ended up in the back in some strange area. We stayed there until the shooting stopped. We heard the police officer's radios so we started coming out. People were laid out all over the place. There were trails of blood, shattered glass and bullet holes on the floors and walls. I went outside and stood across the street watching them bring bodies out praying that my cousins were okay. Around twenty minutes later, my cousins arrived. I could still hear the ringing in my ears from the loud music and gunshots. I saw some

CHAPTER 3

guys sitting in the back of a squad car in handcuffs—-it was just another day in the hood.

Chapter 4

C.I.-Sheepshead Bay, Brooklyn - & No Bat!

Sheepshead Bay & Nostrand Avenue houses had a long waiting list and was predominately white neighborhood. They said if some of my people transferred from other projects it would be a more diverse group of people. Not sure if this was a good idea but it worked for us. My father was so happy when they called us.

I loved my place in Sheepshead Bay. It was a little quieter than Coney Island and much better than Bed-Stuy. There was a supermarket right across the street, as well as a laundromat two blocks from the bus stop and most of my neighbors were pretty friendly. There were a lot of elderly, white people in my building.

Summer time was right around the corner and I continued to spend time with my old friends. I was out with some girls from public-school down at Astroland Amusement Park in Coney Island in front of the Polar Express. They started playing all the Jams. Slick Rick, Beastie Boys, Eric B and Rakim, Special Ed, etc. So as usual everyone started battling each other.

"Go Toya, Go Toya, Go Toya." Everybody gave me high-fives after I finished dancing.

"There she go, yeah that's her." Monique mumbled to her friends.

"Oh, so you think you can dance? Look at her fake Michael Jackson jacket."

"Don't touch me." I said as I moved my shoulder away so they didn't touch my jacket.

"Oh, and she think she bad. — So, this is the girl that was staring at you?" Monica asked Monique.

"Yeah I was on the train and I fell asleep and when I woke up she was all in my face. I looked at her like, what? Then she looked back and shook her head." Monique crossed her arms against her chest.

"What you shake your head for?" Monica asked.

"Because she had on a jacket with a matching hat from CVC and I had just had an argument with someone, telling them they were in that program. So, I wasn't staring at her I was looking at the logo." I rolled my eyes at them.

"Who you getting smart with?" That was Eva.

"Well y'all coming around me like y'all gonna do something."

"Yo, punch her in her mouth, I don't like her attitude."

One of the girls swung at me and we started fighting. I was hitting, kicking, biting, punching and pulling hair. It started with two girls, then three, four, five until a total of twelve to thirteen girls were hitting me. I got two girls that I wouldn't let go of. When we fell to the floor I heard someone say, "Break it up." The police came and asked me what happened? I gave them my side of the story but none of the girls were anywhere to be found.

"Are you okay? We're sorry, we tried to help you but they wouldn't let us through." Amanda said in frustration.

CHAPTER 4

"I understand, is my face scratched up bad?"

"No, just a few scratches, but your nose bleeding."

"That's alright. Y'all hurry up."

"What you gonna do?"

"Go change my clothes. Get my people."

"You not coming back, are you?"

"Hell yeah. This shit aint over."

I got to 2828 Mermaid Avenue, made some phone calls and within two hours, I had almost fifteen to twenty people with me. We walked back to the park and waited to see if we could see any of them bitches that couldn't fight fairly. Around two blocks away I could see a group of people coming in our direction.

"I think that's them." I gasped.

"You ready?" Deanna asked.

"Yeah, I'm ready."

My heart was beating a mile a minute but I was happy I had back up. But at least I knew I would have a fair fight.

"So, where the rest of your crew? It was a whole lot more of y'all a while ago."

They all started snickering. Some mumbled under their breath. The others looked a little scared. Others were ready for whatever.

"You ain't come back to fucking talk." Deanna said. "Fuck her up!"

I put my hands up and we started boxing, swinging, pulling hair, ripping each other's clothes. I heard a lot of people cheering me on as well as her. I looked to my left and my cousins Alisa and Sherri were back to back fighting girls. One of the girl's nose was bleeding.

The cops came riding through and told us to break it up and go home. We went our separate ways. A couple weeks later, we were at it again. I didn't condone fighting; however, you couldn't allow people to bully you and not defend yourself or you would always be a punching bag. I'm small and they thought I couldn't fight. Then when I fought back and held my own, they continued to try and break me down. Yes, I had people who would fight for me but I had to do this myself. The other girl was a lot bigger and stronger, but I was faster.

My sister and brother always taught me how to fight and defend myself. My sister and I used to get physical at times, and that's how I learned when enough was enough. One day I got so upset, I kept telling myself one day I was gonna beat her. Even if it meant beating her at being afraid of something.

"I'm going outside," I said to Aliceia.

"Did you ask daddy?"

"He's asleep."

"Well you need to tell him where you're going."

"I just told you. I'm going outside."

"Outside where?"

"I don't know."

"Who you getting smart with?"

"You." I said as I mouthed the word *Bitch*.

Slap and a loud ringing in my ear was all I could hear. I ran out of the house and went to the Webster's, my second home. Later that evening, I waited until my sister was watching one of her favorite television shows.

"Aliceia, hurry up I need you." I said loudly and like I was afraid.

She ran into the kitchen all frantic.

"WHAT? WHAT? WHAT HAPPENED?" She yelled.

I threw my nicely wrapped cat in a blanket on her. She was terrified of my cat.

"AHHH!!!! OH MY GOD! GET IT OFF ME!" She yelled.

CHAPTER 4

She was screaming so loud the cat got scared too and dug his claws deeper into her chest. Her friend ran in the kitchen and took the cat off of her. I dashed out the door back to the Webster's like nothing happened.

Since I was getting older, I tried not to fight with my sister as much. We may have argued but we didn't hit each other.

I was starting John Dewey High School and I needed to stay focused on my education and find a job. I still got an allowance and I made money doing hair and babysitting. I was undecided whether I should go to Lincoln or Dewey. Then I found out Vanessa and Sherri might be moving to Virginia, so I chose Dewey.

Deidre, Sharon, Devora and Sekina were my other neighbors who went there, so I would know a few people. Deidre showed me around and walked me to my classes. She introduced me to some of her friends. At that time, my father got another apartment on 36th street, which was two houses down from Deidre. It was very convenient being that we went to the same school. Deidre started hanging out on 21st street in this big, peach building called 2007. Being back in Coney Island, I started hanging down there too. One day while we were walking down Surf Avenue, we ran into three of the girls I had beef with.

"There she go. We should fuck her up." Shareen said to the other girls.

"Keep walking Toya, it's just words."

"I should punch her cousin in the face."

"Just keep walking. — As long as they don't touch none of us, we good."

Then a 40-oz bottle came crashing behind us.

"I'm not gonna keep walking."

I turned around and asked Shareen, "What's the problem?"

"You the problem." Monica responded as she tilted her head with an attitude.

One of the girls ran to the trashcan to get another bottle; meanwhile, me and the other girl were scrapping. All of a sudden, I heard tires screeching.

"Get in, hurry up." Ace looked at me, then tapped the side of the car.

After punching the girl in the face one more time, I saw two other guys in the car with the back door open. We talked shit to the girls as we walked away to Ace and his friends.

We hopped in the car and rode off down Surf Avenue.

"Damn, y'all was right on time. But is this a stolen car?"

"You know it!" Ace said as he looked through the rear-view mirror.

"Aww hell no! Let us out in front of 2980."

"Thanks, good looking. We just came from around y'all way."

"Y'all be safe and stop fighting." Lu-Lu said.

"Oh really, they started it."

When I got home and told my father what happened, he was a little upset but not because I was fighting but because they kept picking on me.

"You need to get you a bat."

"What am I going to do with a bat, daddy?"

"Knock a couple of them upside the head."

"And what if I kill one of them."

"Shit, that's self-defense."

"I'd rather use my hands."

"Well let's ride around and see if we see them. I'll hold the little bitch down and let you wear her ass out."

"You a mess daddy."

CHAPTER 4

The word got around to my brother and he was pissed. He got into an argument with one of the girl's brother.

"Yo sis, you alright?" Glen asked. "I heard you held your own."

"Yup, you taught me well."

"You might need something to carry around with you."

"Nah, I'm good."

"Well I'm coming to get you tomorrow night so we can go to the boardwalk."

Taking Glen's advice, I decided to carry a box cutter. If you ran the blade across a raw onion and underneath your fingernails, when you cut or scratched someone the wound stayed open and it took a lot longer to heal, often leaving a scar. Thank God I never had to cut someone, but I was definitely ready. My god-sister suggested I carry it in my mouth but I didn't feel comfortable doing that.

Freshman year was about to end and my school always had a big celebration called the country fair. They had two DJs, t-shirts, buttons, food, non-alcoholic drinks, games and lots of prizes. I had two close friends in my homeroom class named Mickisha and Dawn. I met Mickisha first. We were the only black people in the class so I decided that we should stick together. I introduced myself and we got along great. Mickisha lived in a rough neighborhood in Brooklyn. Brownsville. She had two brothers and a sister. Her mother worked as a beautician and kept Mickisha hair on point. Her mother Myra was very pretty and down to earth. She dressed really nice and her hair stayed styled to perfection.

Dawn lived in Brooklyn as well in another area called Bushwick. She lived in a big house with her mother, aunt, brother, sister and a few cousins. Everyone always made me feel like family.

We started going to house parties. Dawn knew all of the latest dances and whatever we didn't know she would teach us. Dawn stayed to herself at first but once we got to know her, the three of us became the best of friends. We even all went to prom together on a yacht and then partied at Latin Quarters, the night club afterwards.

We all started getting summer jobs in high school. I began working at Roy Rogers Restaurant in Brooklyn after school and on the weekends. I ended up quitting because a lot of the employees were stealing. Once I became a supervisor, it started interfering with the relationship I had with others, including other supervisors that I knew were doing it as well. Then one of the supervisors started messing around with one of the girls.

"Y'all better hurry up so we can catch this bus."

"I got a ride, you can ride with us."

After counting the money and locking up, we got in the car and headed home. We pulled up to her building and I got out.

"I can walk from here, I appreciate the ride. Thank you."

Not even ten steps from the car, I saw a bunch of flowers come flying out of the passenger side of the window. I walked back to the car and noticed other people staring at the car.

"Are y'all okay? Y'all pretty loud."

"You not gonna do me like this, so you fucking her or what?"

Damn, Ronnie's girlfriend found out about the other girl he had been messing with. I was gone before her brother came and started shooting. Too much drama for me so I started looking for another job.

I attended summer school, night school, and I started taking a class on Saturdays at Kingsborough Community College so I could graduate early. I completed all my required courses in the late fall so after winter recess I didn't have to go back to school.

I began working in the main office of my high school so I got a chance to still hang out with my friends, Dawn and Mickisha. Deidre had graduated already and was attending Brooklyn College. I worked

CHAPTER 4

there for about a year and a half. It became difficult juggling school around my work schedule so I quit and started working at Fashions Shoe Store with my Deidre, then we got my other cousin Vanessa a job there as well.

Working and going to school allowed me to start growing into a young lady and I began dating. I met a guy that lived in Coney Island. His name was Black. My cousin Deidre was dating his friend Craig. Black was a lot older than me so I knew my father was going to have a problem. I decided that I would introduce him to the family after my graduation. I already told my brother all about him, and come to find out, they did a bid (jail time) together.

"Daddy I want you to meet my boyfriend."

"What boyfriend?"

"His name is Black."

"How old is he?"

"Huh?"

"If you huh me, you can hear me. You heard what the hell I said. He must be old."

"Only a few years older than me."

"A few is two or three."

"Well maybe five or six."

"Five or six? That nigga old as I am."

"How many rug rats he got?"

"One, a son."

"So, when this Black person coming over?"

"I wanted to wait until my graduation party. Then he can meet everyone at once." I smirked.

My father was working overnight at Pathmark Supermarket on Cropsey Avenue. I was a little nervous talking to him face to face. So, I wrote him a five-page letter explaining why I felt I was ready to take my relationship to the next level. We sat down and had a long talk. That weekend he brought me to the clinic on Neptune and 23rd Street in Coney Island to get checked out and obtain some birth control. Then he told me he wanted to talk to Black alone.

I was so glad that I was making more money at the shoe store and I would be starting college in the fall. I was planning to become a social worker and York College in Queens had a great program. Also, my cousin Lisa and two of my friends from high school, Dawn and Mickisha, were attending as well. The extra money from my financial aid would help my dad with the bills.

"You need to save your money and stop worrying about me. You know me and your mother ain't gonna be here forever."

"I know daddy, I have money saved up."

As a teenager, I wasn't trying to hear that. My parents never got sick, no major health issues, so I wasn't worried. The only thing that bothered me was the excessive drinking and smoking cigarettes. Vodka straight for my father and scotch and milk for my mother.

Black and I dated off and on for six years. He became very close to my friends and family throughout the years. I helped him study and take classes and get his G.E.D. through a program they had at my school. I tried my best to keep him out of Coney Island and out of trouble. He was always fighting and loved the streets. Eventually, Black and I started having problems and we broke up. He couldn't let go of the streets.

My father got a two-bedroom apartment in Sheepshead Bay & Nostrand Avenue Houses. My sister was pregnant with her second child, Beau-Anthony. When we moved, my father allowed her and her family to stay there. She had a good job working as a token booth clerk. Me and my cousin Sherri would go visit her late night, usually between 2:00 and 3:00am. She actually went into labor at work one night at seven months and delivered my nephew. My sister, Junior, and me took turns visiting Beth Israel Hospital on the lower east side in Manhattan, making sure he received as much love as possible. Throughout the months my father started getting sick. He was in and out of the hospital until they discovered he had lung cancer. With my sister having a newborn and another daughter and my brother in jail, it was hard on me to maintain the responsibilities of school, work and taking care of my father.

It was difficult going out trying to enjoy myself knowing that my dad was sick.

"Why don't you go out, I know you miss your friends."

"I don't wanna leave you. I've been gone all day"

"I'll be alright, you got to go enjoy your life. If God take me tomorrow, I'm happy I don't have any regrets, with the exception of your mother."

"Well I'll wait until you fall asleep but I'm not spending the night out, I'll take the cab home."

"Okay, be safe."

Once my dad fell asleep, I got dressed and headed out to Coney Island. I found out there was a party in the Coconuts. Deidre, Tawana and I decided to go. We found out it was a guy's party and D.J. Carter from the pink building was playing the music, so I knew we were good. We saw a lot of familiar faces outside, went inside the building and took the elevator to the eighth floor. I just hoped I didn't run into Black. He got rowdy sometimes and I didn't want to be embarrassed. I had a lot on my mind and just wanted to listen to music and dance.

D.J. Carter was spinning Eric B and Rakim, *I came through the door, I said before I never let the MIC magnetize me before*. We immediately started doing the cabbage patch, the wop and the Fila. We went to the back bedroom and gave our respect to the D.J., then said our hello to the person who gave the party and mingled with the crowd.

Then we saw a commotion at the door. "Nah." Red said. "Y'all niggas ain't coming up in here."

"Oh, it's like that?" Blue asked.

"It is what it is."

"What's up now?" Greasy, *AKA Black* hollered.

"Oh shit, that's Black."

"So, we can't come in?" Black, asked.

"Nah, y'all niggas don't know how to act, plus it's already tight." Quan replied.

"Fuck them niggas, it's another party in 23."

A few minutes later there was another commotion at the door. More guys tried to get in that they didn't fuck with.

"Y'all niggas aint all that. I'll shut this whole shit down."

"Yo, Yo, Yo what's the problem?" Carter asked.

"Why y'all fronting not letting people in?"

"It's a private party."

"I don't like the way you talking to me son."

"So, what's up? —-You came to my fucking door, and we said, NO."

Boom, boom was all I heard as they kicked the door in then left.

"It ain't over nigga we'll be back, y'all gotta leave this mother fucker."

Around thirty minutes to an hour later, we see some guys run in the back, gather up a few more guys, and they all run back out the door. Shit. They were fighting in the hallway. A few minutes later you hear, **Pop. Pop, Pop**. Everybody started yelling.

"TOYA. DEIDRE. OVER HERE." Junie yelled as he flipped over a table holding cups and drinks.

CHAPTER 4

"Y'all stay here. Don't come out until I come back."

He reached behind his back and cocked back a .357. We ducked down and heard more shots. What seemed like forever happened in a couple of minutes. Junie returned like he said.

"Y'all good?"

"Yeah. Can we get the fuck out of here now?"

"In a minute. Hold this."

He handed me the hot smoking gun.

"Put it in your bag. I ran out of bullets."

A few minutes later we all ran out.

"Oh my God, that's Curtis." I screeched and froze in my steps.

A few feet from the door lying in a pool of blood, was Curtis.

"We have to help him." I cried.

I tried to go back to see if he was breathing.

"He's gone Toya. Come on, I got to reload."

He grabbed my hand and we all ran, taking several steps at a time down the staircase. We ran out the building and they were shooting outside. We hid down a ramp on the side of the building. Junie came back to get the gun I was holding with a pocket full of bullets. He reloaded his gun.

"On three I need you all to run toward the street, zig zag through the buildings. Ready? One. Two. Three."

We started running and he started shooting and chasing some guys toward Dwyer Gardens. In the process of all the commotion my glasses fell and people were stepping on them trying to get out of the way. By the time I put them back on, they were all scratched up. The next day we went to see my sister so I could tell her what happened the previous night. Damn! It looked like it was snowing. My lenses were so messed up. I should have stayed home.

Chapter 5

On My Own

There's an old saying when one person is taken away, another one is born. Being an adult had its advantages and disadvantages. You have to learn how to make choices that affected you for the rest of your life. Sometimes I felt like I was growing up so fast. The average 20-year-old was still at home with their parents. My father taught me a long time ago, God bless the child who had her own.

College life was great. I loved the financial aid checks as well. I had been going to a few parties in the school. One other highlight was when I saw my favorite rapper, LL Cool J. He lived in Queens, New York, not far from my school. I enjoyed going shopping on Jamaica Avenue. Being from Brooklyn, I didn't come to Queens often. At my college, the classrooms were huge and reminded you of a movie theater. My cousin Lisa took me on a tour one summer and I finally got to see how huge the campus was. We were both social work majors, so I was a little familiar with where everything was. The food was a little costly compared to free lunch in high school. I hated the long two-hour ride from Brooklyn to Queens. Not only did I have to take two trains but I had to take a bus as well. I met some interesting people on my commute. The things you saw in the subway were unbelievable. You had huge rats that weren't scared and homeless people begging for money.

"Excuse me Miss. Do you have 75 cents?"

"No,. . ."

"Fuck you, bitch!"

"YOUR MOTHER'S A BITCH!" I yelled. "FUCK OUTTA HERE!"

There were pickpockets, flashers, people jumping on the tracks in front of oncoming trains, trying to commit suicide, musicians, singers, people dancing or playing instruments and magicians. Then you had the hustlers.

"Batteries, batteries here!"

It was never a dull moment. You just had to hold on to your pocketbook, earrings and chains, especially during rush hour.

During my sophomore year, my father started taking a turn for the worse. He would wake up coughing so hard at night. One night I got up to check on him. He asked for a glass of water and a washcloth because it was so hot in the house. We had the windows open but it didn't really help much. When he used the rag to wipe his mouth I noticed that there was blood on it. We also started to see blood in his urine. His hair started falling out and he began to lose a lot of weight. My father began taking naps, which was extremely unusual being that he suffered from insomnia. He also started having hallucinations and delusions.

"Where's your mother?"

"Mommy don't live here Daddy."

CHAPTER 5

"Well I'll be damned, she left me?"

"Y'all been separated for some time now."

"She got a new boyfriend?"

"I'm not sure daddy."

"You know. You're just not telling me."

I called my sister and let her know what was going on. We began to take turns going with him to the hospital and taking care of him at home. They finally agreed to give him a home attendant. I introduced myself to her and then to my father. I told her that he could be a little difficult but that he really meant well.

"Who the hell is that?" My father asked.

"This is Myriam."

"What the hell she doing here?"

"She's your new home attendant."

"That bitch older than me, I don't need no damn home attendant. You know they steal."

"Oh my God daddy. You ain't got nothing to steal."

"You a motherfucking lie. I got plenty of shit!"

"Just give her a chance, please?"

"Alright, Myriam, where you from?"

"Jamaica."

"Oh, hell no I don't eat no goat or fish heads. Don't even cook that shit in my kitchen."

"I will only cook what you need sir."

"Don't call me sir. You look older than me."

"Daddy please, I gotta go," I said, shaking my head.

"WELL TAKE HER ASS WITH YOU!" My father yelled.

He cursed the lady out so bad. After the second day, she never came back. I wrote my brother a letter to keep him posted on our father's health, I didn't want to stress him out, but I needed to prepare him for the worse just in case something happened. Despite the pain and suffering, my father continued to laugh, smile, tell jokes and help me with my school work.

One day my sister came over and it was time to bathe my dad. Now this was very uncomfortable for me, but being that my sister's stomach was getting bigger, I had to do it. I ran the water and put some bubble bath inside. We guided him into the bathroom and helped him undress. He stepped into the water.

"Got Damnit! What the fuck you think you doing? Boiling potatoes? That water is as hot as fish grease."

"It's not that hot."

"It is too hot. Add some cold water or I'll bust you upside your head."

I added some cold water, then he got in and I started gently washing him.

"I know you don't wash Black like this. You gotta scrub my balls."

"That's it. I'm not washing you no more."

"Oh, so you gonna let me stay dirty? Before I used to wash your stinking ass."

"Aliceia, I can't. I'm calling your social worker in the morning to get you another home attendant."

"And I'm gonna run her ass out the door like I did the last one."

I just walked out the bathroom and my sister took over. A couple of weeks later they did surgery and removed his lungs, replacing them with plastic ones. As soon as we got home he told me to go to the store and buy him a pack of Winston cigarettes.

"A what? You gotta be joking. I ain't buyin' you no damn cigarettes," I responded.

"Well I'll go myself. I ain't got no lungs, stupid. Smoking can't hurt me now."

CHAPTER 5

"Well the second-hand smoke can kill me. Why don't you smoke some weed? I read an article that said it helps with your appetite."

"What if I get some bad weed? Then I'll be dead or tripping out. I ain't listening to you."

"Well you can just read the articles. I'll print it out at school."

"In the meantime, get my damn Winston's."

I was really starting to get scared. My father has been my backbone my entire life and I just couldn't imagine life without him. I couldn't understand how he continued to be full of life when the doctors repeatedly told us that he had months to live.

The next couple of months were challenging. Going to school full time, and working and taking care of my dad. Even though Black and I had broken up, he was still very supportive. It was difficult for him as well to see my father go through so much pain. One day my father fell in the bathroom.

"Help, I've fallen and I can't get up."

My sister and I ran to the bathroom and he was lying on the floor. When we picked him up, he started coughing blood into the sink. We called 911 and the ambulance brought us to Coney Island Hospital. All the doctors, nurses and orderlies knew my father because he kept everybody laughing. After a couple of days and lots of tests, the social worker met with us and told us about hospice in Mount Vernon, New York. They set everything up for us and we were scheduled to leave next Monday. We rode for a long time. It was maybe two hours to this huge hospital. The doctor stated that the goal was to make the patient's last days as comfortable as possible. The hospital was nice but the atmosphere was dreary. They allowed the patients to smoke and drink alcohol. I wasn't really feeling the place. After meeting several staff, doctors and nurses, it was time for the ambulance service to transport me and my sister back to Brooklyn.

I cried most of the way home. I called my father the next day and he told me that place was boring but not to worry. A few days later, "Y'all come and get me, this place is depressing. I'd rather die at home. I called my social worker and she's gonna make some arrangements for y'all to come get me."

"Okay daddy. We'll be there." I said and hung up.

I was so happy my father was back at home. It was difficult to get him to eat and when he did, it was hard for him to keep the food down. After reading the article he agreed to try marijuana. I called Black and asked him to bring my father some weed. Black rolled a blunt and left it on the table because my father was asleep when he stopped by. The next day when I returned from school, my father was sitting up eating, laughing and watching Good Times. I had the biggest smile on my face.

"Daddy, look at you. How you feeling?"

"I feel good."

"I see you eating. Did you throw up?"

"Nope. You're trying to kill me or something?"

"Huh, what you talking 'bout," I asked.

"I almost coughed up my fake lungs with that cigar you rolled, I only smoke white boys."

"Nobody uses paper anymore, daddy."

"Well, I do, that shit is strong but I forgot how it makes you feel. This some new shit, watch out now."

On my father's next doctor's appointment, he received some good news.

"Well Mr. McCray, I heard you left the hospice."

"Yeah Doc, that place was too depressing."

"Well, do you need another home attendant?"

"No, I'm okay."

CHAPTER 5

"Well, your blood pressure is stable, the lungs sound good. No blockage, and you gained ten pounds. Now I don't know what you're doing, but keep up the good work."

"Thank you, Doc, but I'll tell you what I'm doing. My daughter over here," he said pointing to me as I shook my head from side to side, — "don't shake your head." By now, I was grinning.

"Like I was saying, my daughter been giving me weed. We read this article that says it helps with nausea and I haven't been throwing up." He replied, nodding his head and grinning too.

"We're still looking into that. There are some studies that suggest it. Just keep it up." The doctor said before vanished through the oversized hospital door

With everything going on, I started messing up in school and the dean of administration sent me a letter stating that I would be kicked out of school if I didn't get my grades up. I had to go before a committee and explain why they should allow me to continue my education. I wrote and read a three-page letter on how important my education was to me. I told them a little bit about my background growing up, and then gave them a detailed explanation on what my day looked like working, going to school and taking care of my father. There wasn't a dry eye in the conference room. They agreed to put me on probation.

But after the surgery, things started to go down-hill. My father began to develop infections and within a couple of months of going back and forth to the hospital, he passed away in his sleep at Coney Island Hospital.

I was so happy they allowed my brother to come to the funeral. It was heartbreaking to see him kneeling in front of my father's casket in handcuffs. But as long as he was able to give him a proper goodbye that's all that counted. My brother in-law John, Jr., wrote a beautiful eulogy. Most of our close friends, coworkers, and family members were all in attendance. I still don't know how me and my sister got everything together. I know she paid for most of it out of pocket because unfortunately, my father did not have life insurance. Even though my nephew Beau-Anthony's one-year birthday was approaching, we had a funeral to plan, so we celebrated the following weekend.

My sister moved in with me to help out. After going back and forth to court for over a year, New York City housing authority stated that I was the only person on the lease. By law, they could not put me out but they transferred me to a one bedroom. I explained that I was a college student, only working part-time, but they weren't trying to hear it and moved me anyway. I went and spoke to my housing assistant and she gave me a letter to bring my public assistance. I received a caseworker, and they paid my rent in full, gave me $68.50 in cash and $135.00 in food stamps every month. Plus, I was still working.

I hated living alone, and every chance I got, I invited friends and family over to spend the night. They only moved me up the block, so I was familiar with the area. I immediately started making friends. I met three girls named Lisa, Cassandra and Jackie that went to my old public school. All of them lived in my building.

Me and Black got together mainly for my father, whose dying wish was to make sure that he watched over me. He did good for a couple of years; however, we began to go our separate ways when I started to outgrow him. We remained good friends and often ran into each other.

The next couple of years I tried my best to stay focused on my studies and work part-time. I wanted to work full-time but doing so would require me to pay my own rent, so I decided to allow the system to help me out until I got on my feet. I loved spending time

CHAPTER 5

with my niece and nephews that lived close by. My other nieces and nephews lived in Manhattan. I went to see them when I could catch up with their mother, Laverne.

My sister was pregnant again with her last son Anaje. When he was born, he was nothing like Dakira and Beau. He was mean as hell. He only wanted to be with his mother and father. We had to trick him in order to get him to spend the night at my house. My mother would not babysit him unless my sister put him to bed first and he always woke up, so I was the only one that really babysat for her. Usually the kids loved me but he didn't like anyone, so I didn't feel that bad.

One time, my sister and her two best friend's Deanna and Tracey were going to this party in their building.

"So, Tracey, we heard they having a big party tonight in the center and everybody is talking about it. Can we go with y'all?" I begged.

"Shit, y'all know I don't care but y'all gotta ask Dee and Lee-Lee."

"Now you know we can convince Deanna, but Aliceia gonna say, HELL NO!"

So, we found Deanna first.

"Hey Dee. So y'all going to the party in the building tonight?" Gigi asked.

"Yeah, why?"

"We wanted to know if we could go."

"I don't know, I know y'all growing up and y'all be partying but this party might be a little out of y'all's league."

"Please, we'll babysit for free. —- I'll clean your room." I said.

"I'll do your hair." Vanessa chimed in.

"Let me call Aliceia."

"Oh boy, we can forget it."

Surprisingly, Aliceia said yes and we were ready to party. The only problem was it was an all-black affair and we had to dress sophisticated and sexy. So, we waited until my sister went to Deanna's house to get dressed and the four of us raided her closet. The look on my sister's face was priceless when we walked through the door. Two of the four dresses still had tags on them. I knew I was going to owe her big time.

We had a really good time and the music was good but the food was better. We danced all night and took lots of pictures. The best part of the night was when the D.J. made an announcement to sit the birthday boy in the center of the dance floor and two, exotic, female dancers came out. The men were throwing money like crazy. Now, I had been to a male revue before but I never saw female dancers. They were very entertaining and after seeing all the money they made we had dollar signs in our eyes. After their dance, we followed them into the bathroom. We introduced ourselves and started asking 21 questions.

"So how long y'all been doing this?" Gi-Gi asked first.

"A couple of years." The girl named Legs replied.

"Do y'all work at a club as well?" I asked.

"Yeah, and there's a lot of clubs that need girls."

"Do y'all get to keep all that money?" I asked trying to hide my excitement.

"Yup."

"Where do y'all get your clothes and shoes from?"

"There's several stores you can go to, but we shop in Queens."

"Here take my card and I can tell y'all more."

"We have to do one more set." Legs said as she headed out to the venue.

"Okay, thank you." we said in unison.

I had been on my own for three to four years now. I had two to

CHAPTER 5

three more years left in school and my financial aid was going to run out soon. Me and Gigi looked at each other and said we needed to practice so we could do that shit.

A few days later, I put some songs together that I taped off the radio. Some were slow, some were fast and a few were Reggae. We practiced in my living room. I took some sexy pictures and got some feedback. Then I got a friend of mine to be my practice dummy so I could get this lap-dancing thing down. I would dance in the mirror and perfect my routines to the best of my ability. I was on my way home from school one day and saw Gigi across the platform going in the other direction at Broadway and East New York Avenue.

"GIGI. GIGI." I yelled across the platform.

"Hey girl. She said waving her hand.

"You coming from school?"

"Yeah, where you going?"

"To the gym, I need to get in shape. What you doing Friday?"

"Nothing, I don't have class."

"Meet me at my house around 12pm. I'll call you Thursday to remind you."

"Okay." I said.

I wondered what she had to tell me. When she called me on Thursday, she told me that she started dancing a couple of weeks ago and wanted me to come hang with her at this club. She took me to this place called "Cheetahs." I rode past the spot a couple of times on the bus. Inside it was very colorful. It had jet black with orange cheetah spots all over. At night, the exterior sign glowed bright purple. I decided to just watch. The club was packed. The guys were very friendly and kept asking if I was dancing and what time I went on stage. I told them I was just chilling tonight and that I came to support my cousin. I got a lot of free drinks, a few dollars, and some friendly conversations. Some of the girls were really nice and friendly while others were a little stuck up and standoffish.

Then next time we went out, I took two small tight dresses out of my closet along with a few pair of matching thongs, a pair of heels, make up, baby wipes, perfume and lotion. I neatly put everything in a duffel bag and was on my way. We went to a club in Queens called Gordon's on Sutphin Boulevard. The club was real dark inside, and the walls were black and there were several chairs around the stage with a huge mirror against the wall. There were also waist length bars surrounding the stage to prevent the customers from grabbing you off the stage and a lot of other tables and chairs around the stage. There were a few tables and chairs throughout the club too as well as a bar in the back. The girls had a dressing room downstairs with a few chairs, tables and mirrors. Everybody just chose a spot to put their belongings and there was a girl coming around taking down names. She was like the head of the dancers.

"Y'all need to pay attention. When y'all hear your name, go directly to the stage when the next song starts. No more than 15 minutes onstage or you will be fined."

"How many times you have to go on stage Gigi?" I asked.

"It's Champagne." She said smoothly.

"Right, sorry about that."

"No problem, I might slip up and call you Toya. — Oh yeah, so you wanna audition?"

"Yeah, I think I'm ready. I need a drink first."

"Okay you can wait. We are gonna be here all night. I gave the girl the name Unique for now."

I changed into my outfit, put on my shoes, make-up and nervously tried to remember my routine. I didn't want to wear my glasses on stage, and for my set, I tried to dance without them, but I was very uncomfortable. On my next set, I put on some blue tinted prescription glasses I bought just in case. I observed how the girls went to each guy sitting around the stage and when they got off how they stopped at a few guys at the other tables and the bar as well.

"Champagne, I need another outfit. I only brought four," I said.

"No problem."

We went downstairs and she gave me a colorful dress and a sheer white one-piece short set. Each time I got on stage it got easier and easier and the money wasn't bad at all.

Chapter 6

Momma's Baby

I had changed my name to Alize and then later to Sacred. I went to a club once and there were two other girls named Alize. It was a new drink that came out that started getting a lot of attention. I wanted my name to be unique. Different. Special.

Me and Champagne, who changed her name to Avion, continued to travel throughout the five boroughs: Brooklyn, Manhattan, Queens and the Bronx, and some time Staten Island, but wasn't nothing going on in Staten Island that we knew of. We began networking, meeting other dancers and learning about the world of exotic dancing. We learned some good and some bad. A lot of the predominantly white clubs were picky, and maybe a little prejudiced. If you didn't look a certain way, they wouldn't even let you audition.

"Hi. My name is Avion and this is Sacred. We called earlier about an audition and were told to come in and speak to Tony."

Looking us up and down, the chubby white guy said, "Your hair needs to be past your shoulders. Do y'all have gowns? No two pieces of onesies and you're required to sign up for a gym membership, so come back when y'all ready."

"Damn, that was rude." I said while screwing up my face.

"Don't sweat it. We got two more clubs to check out." Avion said with determination in her voice.

School was going much better. I was able to pull my grades up and maintain in good standards, so my financial aid was not in jeopardy. I wrote my brother and told him, and he gave me his blessing as long as I graduated from college. My sister didn't really like it much, but she didn't judge me for my decision. I told my friends as well. Now, I just had to have a talk with my mother and I could just hear her reaction. It wasn't good. But I decided to call and set up a time to tell her anyway.

"Mommy, I need to talk to you."

"Okay, is something wrong?"

"No."

"Okay. Talk."

"Well, I'd rather speak to you in person."

"Okay. Do you have school tomorrow?"

"Yes, but I'm off Friday. So, I'll come over around 11:00?"

"Okay. That's fine." My mother Harriet said.

Friday rolled around and I took the bus and two trains to East New York, Brooklyn. I rang the doorbell and my mother came to the door all smiles.

"Hey sweetie, how are you?" she asked before giving me a hug and a kiss.

"Fine." I replied trying not to sound nervous.

"You look cute. Where you going?"

"That's what I wanted to talk to you about. I started a new job."

CHAPTER 6

"Aww that's great! Congratulations! Where you working at? Is it far from your house?"

"Let's sit down at the table because you might need it. — It's not that far, and I actually go to different places."

"Okay. Like a salesperson?" My mother replied.

"Not exactly. — I work in a club."

"Okay. Like a bartender or a hostess? You good with people. That'll be great for you."

"Not exactly, Ma. — I'm more like an exotic dancer."

She pulled in her chin.

"What you mean exotic dancer?"

"A stripper Ma."

"A stripper? Oh no Toya, you can't do that. All kinds of drunk men stalking you. What if they follow you home and rape you?"

"It's not like that Ma. They have security and the men can't touch you inappropriately."

"I always knew you loved dancing, but I never thought you would do this. I don't like it. What about school?"

"School is great! Actually a few of the clubs are in Queens, so after school I go to work."

"I still don't like it." she said shaking her head.

"Have you spoke to your sister about this?"

"Yes, she knows."

"And she didn't tell me?"

"I told her I wanted to tell you myself."

"I want to invite you to the club. We can take a cab there and I'll put you in a cab back because I work long hours."

"I AIN'T GOING TO NO STRIP CLUB!" She yelled.

"Well then don't judge or ask me any questions because I wanted you to see for yourself."

There was a long silence that sat in the room. I didn't know what to say and I didn't know what she was thinking. I just knew I wanted to dance.

"Alright that's fair enough." She finally said.

"So what day you wanna come? When you off again?"

"Sunday." My mother said grinning.

"Okay Sunday is perfect because it's slow, so it won't be crowded. We can go around 2:00."

"In the afternoon?"

"Yeah, the club opens at 1:00."

"What time they close?"

"At 3:00am."

"Okay, but I'm gonna talk to your sister first."

"Okay. I love you Ma. — Gotta go shake my ass." I said as I shook my ass in her direction. She smiled.

"Love you too and please be careful."

"I will. You wanna see some of my clothes?" I grabbed my bag and started pulling out pieces before she could respond.

"Sure, Toya."

"Oh Lord. How this go with all these strings?"

"You tie these across your back through these loops then around your neck. These tie around my legs and these are my gloves, G-string and garter belt."

"Wow, that's pretty. I like that material."

"Thanks Ma. Okay let me get out of here. I'll call you tomorrow."

"Okay and be safe."

The following Sunday we got to the club early. I introduced my mother to all my friends, the DJ, the owner Raymone, and a few customers who came in. I was happy that my sister got a babysitter so my mom would feel more comfortable. Customers started buying my mother drinks, and DJ Hype started shouting her out over the microphone. She was having a good time. I walked around the pole quickly then allowed my body to spin around. When I stopped, my mother started clapping. Everybody was laughing and clapping and whistling as well. I climbed to the top.

"Be careful, Toya."

"Sacred Ma, Sacred." I chuckled as I held my self steady while in the air.

"That's my baby. She's good Aliceia."

"I know Ma."

By 4:00 pm it was time to put her in a cab. She was so happy that she came. Her main concern was that I didn't mess up in school and I was determined not to let that happen.

I was always inviting my friends to come hang with me at the club. I always made sure that my sister knew where I was and who I was with. I met this guy named Ty one night at a club called Dreams on Sutphin Boulevard. He seemed like he didn't want to be there, so I made small talk with him and was able to make him smile. He was real nonchalant and didn't seem impressed by any of the dances. I gave him a flyer inviting him to a birthday party we were promoting for one of the bartenders named Carmen. To my surprise he showed up with his friend Booshawn.

"Hey Ty. Glad you could make it." I said.

"I'm here." he said with a warm smile.

"Good to see you."

"You too." He said looking me up and down.

"That wasn't too convincing. You need to loosen up."

"I'm not used to all this. I just got home. I just wanna chill."

"Okay, well chill. You want a drink." I asked.

"No, I'm good."

I walked away to go do a wall dance then I had to go on stage. When I finished dancing I went to change my outfit. I stopped by Ty and his friend to chat for a minute before making my rounds.

"Sacred, let me holler at you. I see you have a lot of customers in here so I won't hold you up. — But I wanna let you know right now, I ain't no trick."

"That's great because I ain't no hoe."

"You said you live in Brooklyn, I hate niggas in Brooklyn."

"Well I don't care for the bitches in Queens, but what that got to do with us?"

"Okay, I'm just saying." He smirked.

Throughout the months we got to know one another and he wasn't as mean as I thought, but he was serious all the time. He never came to the club and made it clear that he didn't like me dancing. Finally, we decided to move in together. He wanted me to move in with him, but he had a basement apartment. I had a one bedroom with more space, so he moved in with me.

I cooked a big dinner and invited my mom, sister and brother-in-law over to meet him. We talked, played spades and got to know one another. I started making plans for my future and decided that I wanted to have one child, graduate from college, then focus on my career and give up dancing. I had been doing this for a couple of years and I didn't want to get comfortable. I told my sister and Ty that if I didn't get pregnant by January 1st, I probably wouldn't have kids until I was comfortably stable.

I got my sister to come to work with me the weekend of my birthday. I had a party at *The Ark* nightclub in Flatbush, Brooklyn on Friday and then Dreams on Saturday. I was praying that my sister didn't get into it with anybody because some of the customers could be a little touchy feely and my sister didn't play that. The

CHAPTER 6

girls were usually cool.

Low and behold, Aliceia had to push this guy for touching her ass. Thank God I knew him, and he apologized and bought her a drink. I went into the small dressing room to change my outfit and there was a dancer named Tropical going off! She had the whole neck rotation and hand motion going.

"I'm tired of bitches coming in here making money with their clothes on and I'm busting my ass on stage."

"Girl it's enough money for everybody."

"That's not the point, Candy."

My sister walked in and asked me, "Do you need singles?"

I was retouching my makeup and I saw Tropical's face all screwed up. I put two and two together. So Tropical went and told the manager and they made my sister pay a tip out fee of ten dollars. She ended up still leaving with money in her pocket and free drinks for me and her all night. I needed to bring her with me more often.

I had been feeling a little under the weather, and on this particular winter day, I felt weak and extremely tired. I sat next to my sister.

"Damn, you hot. How you been feeling?" Aliceia asked me.

"Not too good. I've been a little achy lately."

"I can feel the heat coming off your body. We need to leave now."

"No, it's my birthday, and I'm celebrating."

"Well take these two Tylenols and I'll get you a ginger ale from the store. You might be dehydrated, so drink some water too."

I immediately started feeling better but the next day I was down again.

"You need to take a pregnancy test. When the last time you had your cycle?"

"Ahh, I think— last month."

I took a pregnancy test and it came out negative.

A couple of weeks later I was sick again.

"You need to go to the clinic and take a blood test."

I took another type of over the counter pregnancy test and it was negative again. It had been a couple of weeks and I still was not feeling well. I got to the clinic and they drew blood. The test came back positive. I was not one, or two weeks pregnant, but seven weeks pregnant. I was so scared because I had been doing a lot of drinking at the club. I prayed that it didn't affect my unborn child.

My next doctor's appointment went well and the baby was growing normally. I started losing a lot of weight and I would throw up at least eight to ten times a day. Of course, I had to put dancing on hold. I was literally in the hospital more than I was at home or in school. Ty and I started having problems. I think things were moving too fast.

"Look, I'm sick as a dog all day and night, yet I continue to bust my ass to go to school. If it's too much for you, you can leave."

"Fine Toya, but I told you about your mouth."

"Well if you can't be supportive then go."

"Fuck it then, but I'm gonna take care of my child."

"Whatever Ty, I got too much going on in my life right now to come to your pity party."

Shortly after our big argument, he moved back to Queens. My friends and family were all very supportive, physically and financially. I think it was kind of selfish the way I planned everything, so I didn't stress Ty about it. Being that I had a high-risk pregnancy, I was told to say off my feet, but I couldn't just stop going to my classes, so I would push myself until I would literally pass out.

During this time, my grandmother fell ill, and we discovered that she had colon cancer. My sister, my Aunt Audrey, and me took turns going up to Wyckoff Hospital in Brooklyn. When she got released from the hospital, they sent a social worker to the house, being that

CHAPTER 6

she lived alone. Grandfather passed away a couple of years ago. Every time my sister or I would visit, she would sign the home attendant's timesheet and send her home. She called the agency and told them the lady was older than her and she was afraid that she might fall down the steps and sue her, so she asked that they not send anyone else. But she started taking a turn for the worse, so my mother moved in with her. She would hold my hand and pray, rocking back and forth to the pain. When the Lord called her home, my cousin Doreen and I were both seven months pregnant. The funeral was very emotional, especially since I was expecting, and my hormones were all over the place. My grandparents were members of Grace Baptist Church in East New York, and I remembered going to church many Sundays, especially on Easter.

"Grace will miss Sister Geraldine, as well as the late Bell Johnson. Sister Geraldine never missed a Sunday or Bible Study. She was always very helpful cooking, cleaning and serving the congregation after each service. She would also volunteer at the soup kitchen feeding the homeless. She was such a ray of sunshine that we will all miss shining through this church. We will keep her family in our prayers." The pastor said as he began to eulogize my grandmother.

I started feeling dizzy and I remembered the ushers came over to fan me and give me water. That's all I remember.

It felt weird sleeping in my grandparent's house without them. I always slept in their room with the eight covers on the bed all year round.

"Ma, are you gonna change the room around?"

"No, I'm leaving it just like they left it."

"Well, are you going to throw away grandma's things?"

"I will soon."

"Do you know she still have some of grandpa's stuff in the closet?"

"I know Toya, but I just can't."

"Okay Ma, I'm sorry. When you're ready just let me know."

"Thank you, baby. It just hurts so bad." She said crying.

"I know." I said as I held her tight.

Being that I was getting closer to my due date and I kept waking up in the hospital, I tried to stay at my sister's house more often or kept her kids with me. She decorated her back room just for me with colorful teddy bears that my brother got me from Astroland and Disney curtains that she made. I couldn't believe that me and Anaaj had gotten so close. I was sitting on the love seat while my sister was cooking and he joined me.

"Turn your head." He said.

"What?" I asked, looking confused.

"Turn your head." He said again, as his little hand pushed my chin to the right.

He lifted my shirt up and put his hand on my stomach, and every time he did it, the baby moved. Then he laid his head on my stomach pressing his ear against my belly. If I tried to turn around he pushed my face the other way.

Soon I found out that I had been going into premature labor. Every time I started having contractions I had to go to the hospital and they had to give me a spinal tap by sticking a long needle into my lower back to stop the contractions. This pregnancy was taking so much out of me. My attitude was changing, I felt snappy and irritable all the time. My sister and friends gave me a nice surprise baby shower behind the building of 2828. I almost didn't go because my mother brought me this outfit that I didn't want to wear. Then my baby daddy, Ty, came getting on my nerves and I just wanted to lay down. Then I sent my brother to the fruit stand near Stillwell Avenue Train Station over an hour before and he never came back. I was

CHAPTER 6

hungry, tired, and my feet were swollen. And to top everything off, I kept having a weird craving to smoke a cigarette.

The baby shower was amazing. I had so much stuff that we got stuck in the elevator. I had to leave half of my stuff at my cousin's house because all of it would not fit in the cab. I had one month to go but my doctor said it looked like I might give birth before my due date. Then one night I kept tossing and turning, so I got up and took a shower. I laid back down. About an hour or two later, I was up again. I made sure my overnight bag was by the door and I attempted to go back to sleep. I waited until the sun came up then I called a cab and went to my sister's house. I knew the kids would be getting up for school.

When I got to the house. I couldn't even make it to my room. I just sat on the loveseat in the dining room area.

"Aliceia, I need a bucket." I gagged.

"Here. Take this wet washcloth. You sweating like crazy." She said.

"I feel like I gotta poop."

"Come on Kira, I need to get you to school."

"I can walk with my friend. Aunt Toya don't look so good." Kira said.

"Well, let me walk you downstairs."

"Come and get me from school if she has the baby." Kira said smiling and getting excited.

"Nice try. — See you later."

"Okay Ma, give Aunt Toya a hug for me."

"I will."

I went back and forth to the bathroom but nothing happened.

Knock, Knock, Knock

"Are you okay in there?"

"Yeah, I need the bucket."

I began throwing up on the floor. Then I started crying.

"I'm sorry." I cried so more.

"Don't worry about it. I'll clean it up. Um Toya, I think we better call mommy."

My mother said that she was on her way. She lived approximately twenty to thirty minutes away by cab. My brother was supposed to be back over an hour before and my brother-in-law wasn't home. I refused to go to the hospital alone so I endured the pain until someone else showed up. My sister started timing the contractions and they started getting shorter and shorter. A sharp pain hit me in my lower back and I dropped to one knee.

"I'm calling 911 Toya because your contractions are less than ten minutes apart." Aliceia said nervously.

Surprisingly when the ambulance arrived, my brother and brother-in-law arrived as well. As the EMS drivers were getting information from my sister, my mother pulled up in a cab. The hospital was only ten minutes away, but it felt like an hour. The ride was so bumpy and loud from the sirens. I had never been so happy in my life to see Coney Island Hospital, especially because this time I would not be going home.

When I arrived, they took me right upstairs to labor and delivery. Once the doctor examined me, I was told that I had dilated two centimeters, so I had eight more to go. They suggested that I walk around to speed up the process, putting an I.V. in my arm. I kept telling everybody that my heart hurt and they said it was because the baby was turning and preparing to come out of the birth canal.

"Well if the baby is coming out of my birth canal, why isn't my birth canal hurting? That has nothing to do with my heart."

"What did you eat today?" My doctor asked.

"Nothing. I tried to eat cereal but I threw it up." I said holding my stomach.

"It could be heartburn."

"Heartburn is a burning sensation, this don't burn. It's painful like I can't breathe."

"Just relax. It will be over soon. —- It could be anxiety. Is this your first child?"

"Yes."

My mother and sister decided to get some coffee being that they both worked a night shift and hadn't been to sleep yet. When they came back, the doctor asked who would be in the delivery room with me because I had dilated to ten centimeters. My sister decided to come in because my mother was with her when she gave birth to her oldest daughter and I was there with my sister when she was having her youngest son. I remember promising myself that I would not be obnoxious with all the yelling and screaming. I prayed that I didn't lose control like my sister did. Every time she had a contraction she would yell, scream, and curse out the doctor. She grabbed me by the collar of my shirt and demanded that I take the baby out because I had a Lamaze certificate. She was shaking and pulling on the guard rails to her bed so hard that she broke them. I tried to get my mother and brother-in-law to switch out with me but she cursed them out as well.

"Just slap her." My mother said humorously.

"Slap her? I'm not slapping her Ma. Really? That's the best advice you can give me?"

"Well that's what I did when she had Kira."

"Well, I don't think that's the best solution."

I tried praying with her, wiping her forehead with a wet cloth, feeding her ice-chips, telling jokes, dancing, rubbing her back, but nothing worked. I was so happy when the doctors arrived and she started pushing. So being that I went through that horrible experience only over a year ago, I knew what not to do. I was there with my cousin Vanessa as well when she had her second daughter Shakeya and she did great.

We got into the operating/delivery room and it was very spacious, everything was all white, with bright lights and it was freezing cold. They transferred me from one gurney to the table and had me slide down and put the back of my thighs in some stirrups. They covered the top part of my body and the doctor examined me. He got a razor to shave me then told me to breathe and push when he said push. There were two other nurses in the room as well. My sister was holding my hand and rubbing my back. We went through this pushing for quite some time but nothing was happening.

"Okay mommy, when I say push, push and don't stop. Every time you stop, the baby goes back up. The baby is right there and ready to come out. Now if you can't push it out, we'll give you a C-section and take it out for you.".

"No, I'm a dancer and I don't want any scars on my stomach." I said trying to sit up.

"Well my little dancer, you better get to pushing."

I was too exhausted to push.

"Okay, push."

Then I pushed with all of my might and suddenly I heard...

"STOP! STOP! STOP!"

The doctor was yelling at the top of his lungs.

"What's wrong? Aliceia look!"

"No." She whispered back.

"Yes, go look." I begged her to see what was going on.

My sister's eyes were as big as two saucers. I knew something

CHAPTER 6

was wrong, but I also felt like the baby was out because the pain had definitely decreased. The nurse had to unwrap the umbilical cord twice from around my baby's neck.

"Okay mommy, push." The nurse said.

I pushed one more time and again, nothing. The doctor got on the table with me, and he opened me up. He took a scalpel and cut me up and down then side to side. One more push and the baby came out. The shoulders got stuck and the head was sticking out but I was too small to get the shoulders out so they had to cut and fold the shoulders together.

"Is it over?" I asked.

"Not yet." The nurse said as she tried to assist the doctor.

After a few more minutes, they attempted to put the baby on my chest and the baby was covered in slime and blood.

"Oh no, what's all that stuff?" I asked weakly.

They asked my sister if she wanted to cut the cord, and between sobs she said, "No." After they weighed the baby, sucked all the mucous out his ears, eyes, nose, and mouth and counted all the fingers and toes, they wrapped the bundle of joy in a blanket and brought the baby to me. I was exhausted so I told them to give the baby to my sister. The doctors started whispering and asked me if I was okay.

"Yes, I'm fine. Just tired."

It was a boy, six pounds seven ounces, 33 inches long. He had a head full of hair, beautiful brown skin and purple lips. He already had eyebrows and eyelashes. I was so proud of myself for having him naturally without medication. I did not shed one tear until he came out. I was so happy it was over. The miracle of childbirth was an amazing experience.

I had a little get together at my house a couple of weeks later so everyone could meet the baby. My friends and family were all very supportive. We were truly blessed. I decided to breast and bottle feed. The breastfeeding hurt like hell, so I definitely wasn't going to be doing it for long. Within three months I stopped because I had to go back to school. After my six-week checkup, I received a clean bill of health and decided to surprise my friends at the club.

I dressed my son Tyheem as a pumpkin for Halloween. We went to a Halloween party in 2828 in the community center. Later that night my sister watched Tyheem and I returned to the club. I spoke to the bouncer and asked him to call the owner Raymone to the door.

"Hey Sacred, how's the baby?"

"The baby is fine. I had a beautiful boy."

"Well I wanna work today but I want to surprise the girls. Who's here?"

"Tangy and Candy."

"Okay don't tell anybody I'm here. I'm gonna put on my Halloween costume and surprise them."

"Okay mommy, tell Carmen I said give you a drink."

I went and talked to DJ Wayne and let him in on the secret. I told him to call me by the name Red to throw the girls off. I went in the back and changed into my outfit putting my belongings in a locker and I noticed some of my friends entering the club.

"Who's that? She kind of reminds me of Sacred."

"Yeah, she do, what did she have?"

"I think a boy."

I was almost finished with my set when I climbed to the top of the pole, I gripped the pole between my legs, I dropped my head back to slide down and pulled my mask off. Everyone started clapping and throwing money. I got off the stage and started hugging everyone. After I changed outfits, I showed everyone pictures of my beautiful son.

Chapter 7

Tough Good Byes

I named my son Tyheem after his father. His real name was Tyrone but everyone called him Tyheem. His middle name was Jorge after my father who spelled it George, but I changed it so his name could be TJ if people had a hard time remembering Tyheem. Everyone started calling him Ty for short and it stuck. He was such a happy baby, always smiling and hardly cried even if he was wet or hungry. My mother advised me not to leave him with too many people for this very reason because she knew I was always on the go.

I had his first birthday party at my grandmother's house in East New York. She had a huge backyard and my sister got a pool to add for the party. My mother and sister were doing a great job keeping the house up since my grandparents passed. My mother sometimes lost her patience with the kids so I knew my sister would not be staying there too long.

School was going great. I was a senior and my sister helped me with Tyheem and his father took him sometimes on the weekends. Graduation time was approaching and I couldn't wait to put my degree to use. I would be the first one in my family to have a college degree. I knew my father was looking down at me, smiling from ear to ear.

Graduation day was rainy, so we had to use tents to cover everybody during my graduation ceremony. It was held on our campus, and rain or shine I was walking across that stage. The ceremony was long and a little boring, but I got emotional towards the end. The best part was throwing our hats in the air even though I didn't throw mine because I wanted to keep it as a souvenir. I still had my red one from high school and my blue one from junior high school. We went out to eat at one of my favorite spots in Queens called *The Landmark Diner*. We were able to get the back room because I went there all the time and it was a special occasion. We literally had the place to ourselves. We laughed, talked, ate, and took lots of pictures. I loved my family and was so happy that they could all share my special day with me. All the kids were on their best behavior, thank God because I did not want to hear my mother's mouth.

After graduation, I was blessed to get a job at a daycare center in Queens. One of my classmates was the director and I helped her out in one of our classes. I deliberately took this class at the end of my studies because everyone told me how difficult it was. It wasn't the work so much, but it was because you were required to handle a baby rat and teach the rat an experiment that would enable him or her to learn how to press a lever to make food come out. I was not afraid of rats, but I sure didn't want to touch one. When they were small it wouldn't be too bad but eventually it would get bigger and bigger.

"Girl, I am so nervous I don't think I can do it." Isbeth said.

"I really don't want to do it either but I need this class to graduate so I don't have a choice. Why you taking it?"

"I never received my diploma because I was short a few classes. I'm a director and now it's a requirement. It will also result in a pay raise, so I'm here."

"Oh okay, well I'm Toya."

"Nice to meet you. I'm Isbeth."

We continued to get to know each other throughout the semester, studying together, having lunch together and talking about work.

"So, what you plan on doing after graduation?"

"I'm not sure but I know I want to work in my field. I hear a lot of people say that don't work in the field their degree is in. Do you plan on staying at the daycare center?"

"Oh yes, I'm not going anywhere."

"I applied for a job at the daycare center my son goes to. I filled out the application and got my fingerprints back and they never called me back. Right now, I've been dancing for three years and I'm not trying to make a career out of it even though the money is good."

"I know it is but you can't do that forever. He needs benefits. You have a child."

"I know." I replied.

"Well we're going to have an opening in the summer. You should fill out an application if you're interested."

"Oh, I'm very interested." I said with a warm smile.

"Okay then, well I have your number so I'll let you know when we start interviewing."

"Okay cool. Now let's pass this class."

We were both excited when we passed the class. After graduation, I brought a copy of my resume to her, and she arranged an interview. I was hired on the spot. Most of the children were well behaved. The teachers were cool, and some were older than me. Everyone had been there for years. The commute started to get to me some days, especially in the winter. Some days I had to work from 9 to 5 and others from 8 to 4. When I was in school or at the club, I was able to make my own hours. After a year, I decided to resign and look for something closer to home. My sister was also looking for another job, so I wouldn't have a babysitter. Because it was convenient, I went back to dancing, and saved my money. I also started taking city examinations such as the post office, corrections, police officer, and anything in social services, like caseworker, childcare worker and at shelters. While taking one of the many exams, I ran into a familiar face.

"Excuse me, do I know you from somewhere?" I asked.

"You look familiar but I can't put my finger on it." The man said.

"What school did you go to?"

"I just graduated from York College last year."

"That's it. Abnormal Psychology. Professor Stevenson's class."

Her name was Karen and we sat not too far from each other in class.

"Exactly."

"What you been doing since graduation?" Karen asked.

"I've actually been looking for another job. I was at a daycare center in Queens." I said.

"Well, what you looking for now?"

"Something more like counseling, social work, working with teenagers, pregnant teens, shelters or even another daycare center, but just as long as it is closer to home."

"Oh okay, well I'm going to be leaving my job soon. It's a residential center for at risk teenage girls."

"Oh, that sounds like something I would definitely be interested in."

CHAPTER 7

"Okay cool. Here's the number. The coordinator's name is Michelle. Tell her I referred you. I'm sure you'll get an interview."

"Thank you so much." I smiled and reminded myself to think positively.

"No problem. I know how hard it is." Karen said.

I did my research and I was very interested. The position was for a child-care worker in a group home. They didn't have a full-time position, so I would work per-diem (part time), which was okay with me. I finally had the opportunity to put my degree to use. A lot of teenagers faced a lot of peer pressure and psychological issues. The younger generation needed a lot of guidance, and the older generation was set in their ways and thought they knew everything. The teenagers were stuck in the middle. Therefore, this was my target population.

When I got the job, I used to take the girls on outings. We would also stay up watching movies and talking. I would braid their hair and we would do each other's nails. The girls went to school during the day with a certified New York City teacher. I enjoyed helping them get through the struggles of life, assisting with managing them and preventing them from hurting themselves. Each staff had assigned up to three to four girls, who you would sit down with and counsel. It was the staff's responsibility to document what was said, goals that were set and what the child needed to work on in order to return home or advance to an independent living placement. I was also able to go to court sometimes and support the young ladies. Most of them were sent from the court system, either from school or from parents, obtaining a parent's in need of supervision warrant. If the girls did well they were able to go home, if not, they were sent to a residential treatment facility or residential treatment center for substance abuse. I worked at a diagnostic residential center.

I stayed at the job for six years. I met some really cool people along the way: Vicky, Carla, Sequana, Tyese, Trina, Sharna, Diane, Beverly, Michelle, Marie, Lashwanda, April and Sherine, just to name a few. My favorite was the receptionist Ms. Mary. We had three floors and the third, fourth, and fifth floor was an independent home called Marian Hall. After my first five years of service, they had a big ceremony where we received awards. Presenters gave speeches, we ate great food, and guest speakers shared positive words. We also received gifts for being honored.

Every year at the end of the summer we planned a big trip to Six Flags, Great Adventures Amusement Park. We packed lunches, fruit, and juices. All the girls who displayed appropriate behavior were allowed to attend as well as staff. In the fall, we went back for Fright Fest during Halloween. I didn't really enjoy Fright Fest as much.

"Toya, it's really nothing to be afraid of."

"The park is lit up, and you can see everything." Beverly chuckled.

"Well I heard certain areas are dark." I said.

"Just don't go in those areas."

"Do they really touch you." I asked.

"No."

"Don't lie to her. Yes, they do." One of my girls shot back.

"Oh no, I'm not going." I said, shaking my head.

"Please, we'll keep them away from you."

"I don't know. Beverly, what you think?"

"You are cracking me up." My co-worker said as she laughed.

"Well if I get too scared, I'm going to sit in the van."

They had some nice performances such as The Rocky Horror Show, Little Shop of Horrors and of course Michael Jackson's Thriller. Well let's just say I almost peed my pants. We were walking

CHAPTER 7

through the arcade and I could see people running, but I didn't see anyone scary. All of a sudden, a bloody bride was coming my way and we all ran right into Freddie Kruger. I was so scared I closed my eyes holding one of my residents. As the sound of the chainsaw got closer I grabbed her close to me and attempted to hide underneath a big black hearse they had parked inside, which they were using as a prop. I think I would have done much better watching everything from a distance. Up close and personal, I literally ran out of the park. I was glad the other staff and girls enjoyed themselves. I locked myself in the van and listened to music until they were ready to go.

I really enjoyed taking the girls on different outings. Especially on Wednesday, which was for those girls who did really well all week. It was called a bonus.

During this time, my mother started getting sick, which was out of the ordinary for her because she never got sick. A cold turned into the flu and the flu turned into pneumonia. She would get better then get sick again.

"Ma, you really need to go to the doctor because obviously you need antibiotics."

"Do you have some?"

"No, I don't have any. They have to be prescribed. Plus, I don't know how many you might need."

"Well I ain't going to no doctor."

"When was the last time you had a check-up?"

"A check-up for what?"

"An annual exam, Ma."

"What I need an annual exam for?"

"To make sure everything is okay."

"Are you not realizing that both your parents and your husband are gone. You really need to take care of yourself."

"All I have is a cold, flu, or pneumonia. It's all the same thing."

"No, it's not, and if you would have gone to the doctor like I told you, the cold would not have progressed."

"Oh, so now you know everything?"

"No, I don't, but I know that you need to take your health serious if you wanna live."

Finally, she went to the doctor where she was given some medication and was told to take about a week off from work. She started to drink a lot more which was rare, I knew the pain of not having her parents was difficult. After getting sick again, and after taking the medication, the doctor decided to do a series of different tests, which revealed that her immune system was breaking down and that she had cancer. She refused to take her medication or go to chemotherapy and the cancer spread to her brain causing dementia. She eventually started to forget who we were.

"I hope that other lady don't come. She's too rough."

"Rough? How mommy?" I asked.

"She was brushing my hair too hard. She just jealous cause my hair's longer than hers."

"That other lady is your oldest daughter."

"That ain't no daughter of mine."

"Yes, she is."

"Well, I don't like her."

"I know, you love her."

"So, you have any kids?"

"Yes, I have a son named Tyheem."

"Where he live?"

"With me in Sheepshead Bay. Okay Ma, it's time to lay down so I can clean the kitchen and start laundry."

I would show my mother pictures of our family and friends and she would cry, hit her legs, knock shit over, and yell and scream because she was so frustrated that she couldn't remember a lot of things. It was difficult explaining it to our kids because they were pretty young.

"Don't go in the living room with grandma because she not feeling well."

"Yeah, grandma's sick."

"Did you give her some medicine?" Beau asked.

"Yes, we gave her medicine, so hopefully she'll get better soon."

It got difficult for her to walk up and down the stairs, so we separated the dining room from the living room with huge a china cabinet that my grandparents had for years and moved her downstairs. She got a curtain rod and placed some drapes in front of the opening so you couldn't look directly into the living room when you entered the house. I brought my father's port-a-potty over so it would be easier for her to use the restroom and slept on a pull-out caddy bed that was already in there.

"Hey Ma, do you need anything?"

"Just a cup of water."

"Okay, you want ice in it?"

"Just a little and if any of those little bastards come in here I'm gonna snatch their asses up."

"Nobody coming in here, so relax. Aliceia gone get you if you put your hands on her kids."

She had her television and radio if she wanted to listen to music. We gave her a bell to ring just in case we were upstairs or in the basement and couldn't hear her calling us. One day my sister was brushing my mother's hair and she snapped. She turned around and grabbed a handful of her hair and wouldn't let go.

"TOYA! TOYA!" My sister screamed.

"What? Oh my God, let her go, mommy!"

"No, she too rough."

"Okay, I'll brush it, but let her go."

I had to pry my mother's fingers back to get her off of Aliceia. Another time I was doing her nails and she scratched me. As soon as she fell asleep I cut them real short. She started getting so aggressive that I would put her in one of the therapeutic holds I learned in training at the group home.

We would try and trick her into taking her medication by crushing the pills and blending them with different foods but if she tasted the meds she would spit it out. She loved shakes, so we started putting her medication in them. It was so frustrating seeing my mother deteriorate right in front of my eyes. Especially when we had to continue to work and take care of our own kids. But I wish I could have dedicated more time to just be with her. Then just like that she was gone.

"You need to come home now." My sister was on the phone.

"For what Aliceia? I'm working."

"It's mommy."

I felt like my heart had sunk into my chest. Immediately I felt like it was hard to breath. I told my co-worker that I had a family emergency and we called someone to come and replace me. The train ride from Manhattan to Brooklyn seemed so long. I was walking so fast to the house from the station that I tripped over my own two feet. I must have smoked around three cigarettes in five blocks. When I came into the house, my sister was sitting at the kitchen table. No words were exchanged, and we just hugged each other real tight.

"Where's the kids?"

"In the backyard playing."

"Do they know what's going on?"

"No." My sister replied with her head down.

CHAPTER 7

I walked into the living room and just stared at my mother for a few seconds. It looked like she was sleeping. I pulled back the cover and touched her hand then gave her a kiss on the cheek. She was cold and her skin felt tight. The tears rolled down my face as I said a prayer. I walked back into the kitchen.

"What do we do now?" I asked.

Being that it was the Fourth of July, we were told that her body couldn't be moved that day without a doctor's signature. I couldn't imagine leaving my mother in the house deceased for two more days. She must have passed in the middle of the night because rigor mortis had already set in. My sister decided to call a doctor that she knew. He was on vacation with his family in the Hamptons, which was over two hours away, but he agreed to come sign the necessary paperwork. We called 911, and the police arrived first, then the coroners and then Dr. Goodwin. We were so thankful that he took the time out of his personal life to be such a blessing. This holiday would never be the same.

"I saw that on T.V. before. I think she's dead." A little boy outside the house said as the necessary people moved in and out of the house.

"Y'all move from in front of the house."

"That lady died? What happened to her?"

"Get y'all motherfucking asses away from my yard now, asking all these questions. None of your business. Stop being so nosey." I could tell that Aliciea was hurt and angry.

The next couple of days centered around making funeral arrangements and contacting friends and family members. Unlike my father, my mother had life insurance that helped us out a lot. My mother always said if anything ever happened to her that she wanted to be cremated so we picked out two urns to hold her remains.

It was difficult once again seeing my brother arrive to the funeral in shackles. The officers were very nice and allowed my brother to take them off while in the funeral home. One officer stayed by the door and the other a few feet away from my brother. I know it was really painful for him because he didn't get a chance to hug or kiss my mother like he did with our father. We all kneeled down and prayed together in front of a set of pictures we had on display. My mother said she wanted people to remember how she looked when she was living, so we granted her her wish. We played soft music. Her favorite was Gerald Levert so we played a lot of his music.

A lot of people got up and said very kind words about my mother, Harriet. It was depressing that night hearing the fireworks. I couldn't get into the holiday spirit because I was mourning. As I looked into the sky, I wondered if my parents were together. They were probably fussing, laughing, and crying together. It took us some time to clean out her belongings, especially since my grandmother's things were still there as well. We found so much stuff, lots of unopened birthday and Christmas presents and clothes with tags still on them.

My sister was going back and forth between my grandparent's house and her two -bedroom apartment she had in Howard-Houses that she hated. She finally decided to relocate to West Virginia. I packed the entire apartment alone only leaving out some clothes and dishes. She returned a couple of days later with a shiny set of keys to her new house.

"Congratulations. I'm so happy for you. So when can you move in?"

"It's ready now."

"Really?"

"Yeah, I'm gonna leave in the morning, but I need some help with the U-Haul."

"Okay how much do you need?"

CHAPTER 7

"$600.00."

"Really Aliceia? Okay, let's go to the bank so I can get the money. I'll give you $700 for food and gas."

"Thanks, Toya."

"No problem."

The next morning, she rented the U-Haul and we started loading the truck. When everything was securely packed, we said our good-byes and Tyheem started crying uncontrollably.

"Don't leave me Thee-Thee." Tyheem wailed.

Now all the kids were crying and my sister and I were breaking down.

"I can't leave him. Get in the truck Ty." She said.

Tyheem gave me a hug and kiss and ran to get in the truck. I was left standing there confused.

"Tyheem, you sure you wanna go? Mommy can't get you right away."

"Well, school is out. Come get him in September."

"September? Bitch this is June."

"Well you'll have the summer to yourself."

"What about all his clothes?"

"Mail them Toya, Anaaje ain't too much bigger. I'm sure he got a few outfits in my boxes."

"Oh my God, I don't believe this. Okay, I love y'all. Call me when you get there."

I watched in a big blur as the U-Haul pulled off. I was alone for the entire summer. I kept myself busy, working and saving money. I would send packages to them every two weeks full of clothes, toys, books and their favorite snacks. My son continued to go visit every summer for the next couple of years.

In 2000, New York City, Mayor Giuliani, started kicking strip clubs out of Times Square in order to turn it into a tourist's Mecca. Many of the clubs reopened in Long Island under different names. They started making the club owners follow zoning laws which stated that strip clubs had to be 500 feet from a church or school or they had to close down. Then they started attempting to control your contact with the patrons. Some clubs allowed lap dancing or some form of limited contact, while others had a strict distance requirement. These laws started to affect business, but thank God I had a real job. I continued to work at the group home as well as the club. I met some friends in my building. Both of them had children that were the same age as Tyheem. Throughout the years Cassandra and Lisa babysat for me and I would also watch their kids as well. Tyheem was getting a little older and I wanted him to have his own room, so I went and spoke to my housing assistant. Your child is supposed to be seven years old in order to have his own room, but she allowed me to transfer when he was six years old. We found a nice two bedroom on the other side of the projects. There were a lot of elderly white people in my building, and not too many kids; but that didn't bother me. I continued to spend time with my friends. I knew my son missed my nephews but he had a couple of friends from his school that he played with outside.

A couple of years later, I was at the club and I met a guy named Dee. He was very nice, tall, dark and bald-headed. A little too nice for me. Everyone kept telling me that I was being paranoid and to allow a man to treat me the way I deserved to be treated. But on the other hand, my parents always said, "If it's too good to be true, it is."

"Hey Sacred. What you doing Friday?" Dee asked.

"Working."

"What you doing Saturday?"

"I have to go food shopping before I go to work."

CHAPTER 7

"I wanted to take you out."

"Maybe during the week, because I work Friday from 1:00 pm to 3:00 am."

"What about a Sunday, Monday or Tuesday?"

"I babysit my sister's kids."

"Damn, you ain't never got time."

"Well, I can make time but my bills need to be taken care of first, so it all depends on how much I make and what needs to paid."

"I feel you. Well I need to do some food shopping as well. Maybe we could go together?"

"Now that would be nice."

"Okay, so is 1:00 good for you?"

"Between 11 and 1 is good for me because I have to go to work."

So, on Saturday around 11am he called and told me that he was on his way. Around thirty minutes later, he buzzed my intercom.

"Hey, can you come downstairs?"

"I'm on the way."

I got downstairs and he had his daughter with him. They were unloading bags and bags of food.

"I thought we were going food shopping together?"

"I wanted to surprise you and I wanted you to meet my daughter, Imani."

"Nice to meet you, Toya."

"That's Ms. Toya to you." Dee interjected.

Imani was very pretty, tall like her father and very petite. He kissed me on the cheek.

"Now you don't have to work tonight." He smiled.

Another time I was laying in the bed, and I had plans to bring Tyheem to ride his bike but my stomach was killing me. I was in so much pain I could barely move.

"Hey Sacred, it's Dee. What you doing?"

"Nothing."

"Are you working today?"

"No, I'm not feeling well."

"Sorry you're not feeling well, but I wanted to spend more time with Tyheem."

"Well, let me ask Tyheem, hold on."

"That's fine mommy. I wanna go."

"He said okay."

"Alright cool, I'll be there in an hour. Do you need anything?"

"No, I don't have an appetite. I've been drinking tea all morning and taking Tylenol."

"Well I'll be there soon, so you can take it easy."

He brought Tyheem back with a fresh clean shape-up because he had braids. They went fishing and then out to eat. He also surprised me with some professional pictures they took at the studio. It was dark by the time they returned.

We had been dating for two to three months and everything was great. I was home one day recovering from a hangover trying to get myself together, so I could go to work. It was Mother's Day weekend and I planned to spend the day with my sister, working at the club Thursday, Friday and Saturday. We always exchanged gifts.

"Hey Sacred, what you doing this week and don't say working, it's Mother's Day."

"Exactly and I need money to buy gifts. I'm working Thursday, Friday and Saturday, then spending Sunday with my sister."

"Well what day do I get?" Dee asked with an attitude.

"Didn't know you needed a day, but hopefully Saturday."

Thursday and Friday, I did really well so I decided to spend Saturday with Dee. When I first told him that I had to work, he got so pissed off at me that he didn't answer Thursday or Friday night when I called. Finally, he called me on Saturday morning and apologized. I received cards and a huge bouquet of red roses from him and his daughter Imani. We spent the afternoon together then he dropped her off and came back with a bottle. We listened to music, talked for a while and just sat in the living room all hugged up. Then he got real serious. He took my hands and looked into my eyes.

"You know you're very special to me. I'm so happy that you're in my life."

He got down on one knee and pulled out a small box with a gold ribbon on it.

"Will you marry me?"

I started crying and placed my hand over my mouth. It had only been a couple of months. I was shocked and excited at the same time. I immediately called my sister and told her the good news. Shortly after the proposal, he kept stressing me about moving in with him. After a couple of months when my lease was up, I moved to Queens, New York.

His daughter and my son got along very well. He only had one daughter at the house that he had custody of. They shared a room but we discussed getting a bigger place after the wedding, which was planned for the next year. I felt in my heart that things were moving pretty fast, but I was so happy and decided to let my guard down. He began to get a little jealous of my friends, family, and my job. Even the close bond with the kids started to bother him. I would receive phone calls and he wouldn't give me the message. Once we had a huge argument because he didn't want my son to go stay with my sister at the end of the school year.

"You said he goes every year, so why can't he skip this year?"

"First of all, you're asking me this a couple of weeks before he leaves. I would have to discuss it with Tyheem, as well as with my sister and don't forget about my nephews."

"Well I don't understand how they get a say so. They're children."

"Exactly and how they feel matters to me. It's not about me, it's about everyone coming to an agreement."

"You should just tell him he's not going."

"I'm not doing that, and I don't know how you deal with things with your daughter but I talk to my son and I give him choices."

It was finally settled because Tyheem wanted to go and my sister and nephews wanted him to come as well. Plus, Ty had other cousins his age down there to hang with. Since we moved, there weren't a lot of kids his age on the block. And not too many people to hang out with at the basketball court and nothing much to do.

"Dee, it would be nice if you and Imani could come with me to drop off Tyheem."

"I have to work. We have a wedding to play for."

"What about if I talk to Imani and see if she wants to come? I let her talk to my sister and nephews all the time."

"I guess so."

As the days got closer, I noticed Dee was acting real jealous when I spent time with Imani without him. To my understanding, we were supposed to be a team. I loved it when he spent time with Tyheem. When I got home from work, I stopped in the room to hug and kiss the kids. I noticed Imani was frowning.

"What's wrong Imani, you look sad?"

"Daddy said I can't go with you to drop Tyheem off because I didn't answer the phone when he called."

"Okay." —"Why didn't you answer?"

"I was taking a shower because I had an accident on the way home."

CHAPTER 7

"Oh okay, did you tell your father?"

"Yeah, but he still said I can't go."

"Don't worry, I'll talk to him."

When I went to talk to him, he shut me down really quick.

"No, she's not going. End of discussion." Dee said.

"I know you're really not gonna be that petty and not let her go because she didn't answer the phone, Dee."

"That's exactly why she's not going."

"Did you give her a chance? She was taking a shower."

"She should have called me when she got out."

"You're just ridiculous."

"When I say something, I mean it. I guess you don't know me. As a matter of fact, you still got the ticket?"

"Yeah."

"Let me see it please. When is Ty's birthday?"

"On the sixth."

"Okay, I'll make sure I have an ice-cream cake for him."

All of a sudden, I heard a ripping sound. He was actually tearing Imani's ticket into little pieces.

"I can't believe you just did that."

I got up and walked to the kid's room so I could tell them the bad news. Things really started changing. My job called our house one day to see if I could work at the group home and Dee told my supervisor that I didn't need the job anyone. Dee set up an interview for me at another facility where he knew the director. It was also two blocks from his house. Wedding plans were going well and we picked out invitations and invited his family over for Thanksgiving dinner. I became confused when I started talking about the wedding.

"I love weddings. Who's getting married?" His mother asked.

At this time, we were engaged for six months, so something wasn't right. After the encounter with the family, one of his other daughters told me not to do it. I attempted to push the wedding back to buy some more time because I started thinking that this may have been a mistake. Every time I would mention it, he would do something extra special or show me how important our future was to him, so I kept the date. The wedding was beautiful, and we chose the colors ivory and champagne. It was held in Brooklyn at the Masonic Temple. We decided not to use a church or a mosque to show respect for both of our religions. He was Muslim and I was Baptist. Our religious beliefs didn't interfere with our union at all. We had a total of twenty-three people in the wedding party. We went on our honeymoon to Cancun, Mexico. Everything was perfect. I was offered a full-time position at the group home he chose and only danced once or twice a week.

Dee came home yelling and screaming one evening because he had a picture of us hanging on his mirror in the barbershop and a few customers who frequent the club said something to him about it. It was nothing rude or disrespectful, but he didn't like it. So, I agreed to stop dancing. Shortly after the wedding, the jealousy started to get out of control. He attempted to set one of my friends up with one of his friends. They were around the same age and were both single, but my friend kept changing her mind.

"It's funny how your friend Beverly always got time to go have drinks with you or go shopping with you or want you to do her hair, but she can't never meet up with Vee."

"I don't know why she won't go out with him. Maybe she like being single."

"You sure she don't like you? Maybe y'all two used to be together."

"You gotta be kidding me. We are friends and just friends. Not all dancers mess around with each other."

"Well, I'm just saying something ain't right."

Then he started complaining about the way I treated his daughter.

"I don't know about you taking Imani school shopping. She doesn't need a bunch of overpriced designer clothes. She go to school to learn, not to attend a fashion show."

"I understand but everything doesn't have to be name brand. You can find designer clothes on sale. I do it all the time."

Then he started complaining about the way I dressed. We took turns washing clothes and whenever I got something new, I always bought for the kids as well. We had planned on going to a little cookout at this garage where he hung out with some of his friends. He called and told me he was on his way, so I got a dressed. I put on a pair of Capri jeans, some Tommy Hilfiger slide-ons and a halter top to match. He walked in the room and started getting out a change of his clothes. He glanced over at me.

"I know you not wearing that."

"What's wrong with it?"

"You going to a cookout. You're too dressed up."

"Okay, I can change."

I went into the bathroom with a new outfit and when I came out, I discovered that this nigga left me. So, I called him and cursed him out.

A couple of months passed and it was one of my co-worker's birthday so we decided to go have a drink or two after work when we got off at 11pm. Dee continued to blow my phone up, calling every 15 to 20 minutes. I told him that I would not be out long. After the fifth of sixth call, I just stopped answering. When I got home, he was sitting up waiting for me.

"I told you I wasn't gonna be long. You didn't have to wait up."

"Don't you think it's a little disrespectful to go out with your single friends until one in the morning? You're a married woman now."

"Okay I understand. Patrice is married. Beverly is divorced. Lashawnda is in a long-term relationship. That doesn't mean I can't go out."

"Well it's not respectful for a married woman."

"Okay, Dee."

I went to check on the kids forgetting that my son was out of town and his daughter was at her aunt's house. I began to laugh to myself.

"Oh, so you find this funny?"

Ignoring him I went in the bathroom to take a shower and change into my nightclothes.

"So, you find this shit funny?" Dee asked again.

I didn't respond so he said it a third time.

"What's so funny?"

"You're funny." I said as I smiled.

Before I knew it, he had jumped up off the bed and wrapped his hands around my neck, squeezing my throat. I started hitting, punching and scratching his arms, face and chest. He threw me on the bed. I tried to grab something to hit him with off the nightstand. We struggled on the bed until he was able to pin my arms down near my inner thighs. I was on my back, and his body was on top of my chest. His hands were still wrapped around my neck, strangling me. He began to talk to me in a calm voice, smiling and smirking the entire time. I struggled until I was weak. I began to cry and said the Lord's Prayer at the same time. I began to lose consciousness, and the room started getting dark and I began to see my mom and dad. I thought I was dying. All of a sudden, a strength came over me and I was able to slide my body down a little by wiggling and my foot was able to reach the dresser. I started kicking the dresser as hard as I could until it started to shake, then it finally tumbled on top of us. When he released his grip, I fought my way from under him and the dresser, grabbed my purse and ran out the room, out the double doors, through the gate, down a flight of steps, running for my life. I didn't stop until I reached a cab station. I called his aunt and explained what happened. She gave me her address and I proceeded to go to her house. She was the closest person to me and I needed to get away fast.

Early the next morning, I woke up and I swore I heard his voice. I took my pocketbook and hid under the bed. Later that night, we talked on the phone and he came to pick me up. I had to wear my glasses because my eye was swollen and it was irritating my contact lenses. He cried and apologized, swearing that he would never put his hands on me again. I agreed to take him back on one condition.

"First, we need to go to counseling."

"Okay that's fine I can call Pastor Iman in the morning. Whatever you want."

"You gotta stop with all this jealousy. I have friends and family and we are close. You have to understand that."

"I understand, but I just love you so much. You're right and I apologize."

"I don't care what the Bible says, what the Qur'an says, your mama or the pastor says, you got one more time to put your hands on me and I'M GONE!"

The next couple of weeks were great until he started that jealous shit again. He did his best to keep me all to himself. He even got my name tattooed on his chest, so in return, I got his name on my arm. We talked about getting a bigger place but that never happened. One of my friends had relocated and was coming in town for New Year's. We made plans to hang out, and we went out that Friday. When I came home, he was acting like he had a problem with me. I decided to start putting money aside and take some extra clothes with me to work just in case I had to stay away for a few days. The next day me and my friend went out again because she was leaving on Sunday. I came home around one or two am. He started fussing with me, and we argued back and forth. I started thinking about the last physical altercation we had just a few months ago. So, I went into the kid's room to wake my son up. I started to pack his belongings, but whenever I took clothes out the dresser drawer, Dee would put them back. I went into our room to pack some of my stuff and he kept trying to grab me. I pushed him and called the police. They arrived quickly and told me that I had thirty minutes to gather all my belongings. I tried to explain to the officer that I needed more time. She repeated aggressively, "You got thirty minutes." As I packed frantically, they filled out a police report. I called my sister-in-law crying and she knew a guy with a minivan. I put as much stuff as possible in the van and never looked back. I attempted to get in contact with his daughter, but he told the school that I was not allowed to visit. I tried calling but he would not let me talk to her. She always said that she would find me when she was 18 years old. She never did.

It was a cold winter. Winter recess was soon over and the kids were back to school that Monday. I had to take off to discharge my son from school in order to register him in another. I needed a babysitter and a new apartment. Dee continued to call my phone, my job and when I didn't answer, he started threatening me. It got so bad that I had to get an order of protection. It was quickly granted once the judge heard the messages that I saved. I went to court because he got over $600 worth of parking tickets on his van, and the registration and insurance were in my name. After hearing my story, the judge ordered me to pay half. I attempted to have a tow truck tow the van but he blocked the van in with his other car so that didn't work, and he threatened to sue the tow truck company if they caused any damages.

He refused to let me get the rest of my belongings, which he put in the garage. He also changed the locks. He agreed to let me get my things on my birthday at 1 o'clock. I had my brother-in-law with me but I couldn't get in. I knocked on the next-door neighbor's door and he let me in. I kept feeling someone was staring at me and noticed Dee peeking through the blinds. I ended up losing a lot of stuff, mostly my personal items like photo albums, clothes, winter stuff and books. I felt bad leaving his daughter, but he never mistreated her in front of me. I felt like he was a little tough on her, but as long as he didn't put his hands on her, I understood. She was a straight A student, very respectful and I guess he was only trying to protect her.

When I went back to court, he didn't show up; but because he worked off the books and everything we had was in someone else's name, I still couldn't get anything because on paper, it looked like he didn't exist. The next month I began my divorce proceedings. I was in tears the day I got a phone call from my lawyer stating that it was finalized.

The threats started getting so bad that I had to relocate. It was very emotional saying goodbye to all my friends, family and co-workers. My job gave me a going away party that was more sad than festive. We agreed to keep in touch. With Georgia on my mind, I was on my way to a new start.

Chapter 8

Welcome to Atlanta, GA!

I decided to leave when school got out in June. My son already got held back from the constant moving from place to place because it was affecting his schoolwork. The threats were getting out of control and I needed to protect me and my son. I knew nothing about Georgia with the exception that The Color Purple was filmed out there somewhere, but that's where I was going.

I wanted my son to go first, so I could work a little longer and save money but the state of Georgia would not let my sister register him for school, so I had to call his father. He was livid. I flew to Georgia, rented a car, drove to Virginia and back down to Georgia so I could drop the car off and get back on the plane to New York. I was exhausted.

I felt a lot better with my son being out of harm's way. Fourth of July weekend, of all the holidays, I made the move. My sister had a friend of hers pick me up. The drive was around twelve to fourteen hours. My niece was still living in Virginia, so she picked Tyheem up for me and brought him to Georgia. I decided to enjoy the rest of the summer and started looking for work in August when Tyheem started school. It was going to be difficult getting used to a whole new way of living. There were a lot of differences between Atlanta and New York.

In New York, they started school in September and finished by the end of June but in Georgia, they started school in August and finished in May. I went to the public library to look up some job opportunities online, but nothing changed in that department. So, I went to the department of labor. In Georgia, they contact the person for you and set up an interview if they're interested in you. I noticed a big mental institution right down the block from the house. I looked up some information and it was right in my field of study. It reminded me of a place in New York called Creedmoor. I walked there on Monday and filled out an application to return it on Thursday. I had two interviews before I got hired four months later. I saw a couple of other positions I was interested in but without a vehicle it was impossible to get to and from work on time because the buses and trains only ran until midnight. You have some areas with no public transportation at all. In New York, New York City Transit Authority ran 24 hours a day.

Tyheem was adjusting well, with no problems at all. The people in Georgia were much friendlier than in New York. People would sometimes speak to you more than once in the same day. Growing up in big city like New York taught you not to be so friendly. There were a lot of mean, evil people in New York City, who sometimes pretended to be lost so you could trust them then they would rob, rape or even kill you. There were also a lot of pickpockets, so you could never let someone you didn't know hug you. The food was also different. New York had a lot of cheap fast food restaurants and most

CHAPTER 8

of them were open until one or two am. The clubs in New York also stayed open later. There were a lot of bars and other establishments in Georgia that opened early, but closed early as well. There were no yellow cabs, gypsy taxis, or what we called in New York, dollar vans in Atlanta.

One time, I got kicked off of the bus in Georgia for cursing while I was having a heated argument with my son's father on the phone. Also, if you threatened another person and they had a witness, they could press charges on you because it was considered a terroristic threat. You could also be arrested. In New York, the officers let you fight. In Georgia the laws were way more strict, and they would actually lock you up for drinking with a suspended license or no license at all. Summer time in Atlanta was extremely hot. So hot that at certain times of the day you wouldn't see many people outside. It could be 100 degrees in New York and the parks and streets were always full of people. The winters were also different. New York got very cold, and I mean so cold that you would feel like you had gotten frostbite after walking around. With inches on top of inches of snow we continued to go to work, and school if it was open. We even played in it outside. In Georgia, you might have seen a few flurries here and there but it rarely stuck to the ground and once the sun came out it melted.

In New York, the apartments had hard floors and the walls were thick like concrete. In Georgia, the apartments were carpeted, had a dishwasher, central air in the summer, and heat in the winter, which you could control. In New York, we used fans in the summer and the heat automatically came on in October. In Georgia, you had to pay for trash removal and water. However, in New York, we used incinerators for garbage and water was free.

The cost of living was much higher in New York, so the pay rate was higher as well. When it rained a lot, you had lightning and thunderstorms and the lights would go out in Georgia. Georgia also had a lot of flooding because water collected in trenches and the more it rained, the more built up you had, which caused flooding. Also, a lot of the power lines were all tangled amongst the many trees that surrounded the city. Strong winds would knock your internet and cable service out easily.

I was only working weekends at the time. I worked 12 hour shifts from 8:00 am to 8:30 pm. My coworkers were cool. I had a lot of coworkers that I spent a lot of time with but one that I particularly enjoyed spending time with. His name was Trahern but everybody called him Tray. He was from South Carolina and we had both been looking for another job.

I called him my office spouse since we worked together every weekend and spent time together outside of work as well. I loved going to karaoke with my friend because he could sing his ass off.

I was talking to another coworker and she told me about this hospital she worked at that was hiring. She said she didn't know if I would be interested in it because the patients could be very aggressive at times. That didn't bother me at all. After doing my research, I was even more intrigued. She gave me the information and I applied. They called me in for an interview. The place was huge, and the people were friendly. It was on a bus line, and there was an opportunity for advancement. I received an acceptance letter and was told to report to pick up some information for a drug test. I was given a schedule for one-week training. Training was fun. I received an abundance of information, and CPR and first aid training. I was even allowed to tour my unit.

By day three, I was just about ready to get on my unit and work. My coworkers were all cool and the kids were interesting. They all had their own personalities with similar backgrounds. It was our job

CHAPTER 8

to use their treatment plan to help them either return home or move on to another facility. I was loving my new job. I had to cut my hours short at the group home because I was required to work every other weekend at the hospital. I was told that I must work at least one 12-hour shift in three months to keep my job and that wasn't a problem.

Soon I began to make friends at the hospital. One of my closest friends, was Takiyah. She was from Massachusetts and was very down to earth and fun to be around. Ebony was from Massachusetts as well. I learned a lot from her on how to deal with the kids as well as some staff. Dusell, was from Harlem New York, still had that New York attitude that sometimes-intimidated people, and I loved it. She kept it real all of the time. Wiltonia was from Texas, and she was my ride or die chick. Nobody fucked with her and she didn't really mess with too many people at the job either. She had a great sense of humor and kept me laughing. Alohma was from Carol City, Florida. Her son and my son are a year apart and they spent a lot of time together. She had an apartment in the same complex where I lived so we carpooled and hung out together on our days off.

Interestingly, I noticed a man at my job, Travis. Travis had that New York flavor that was irresistible to me. He was dark skinned, with smooth skin and had a warm smile, but you could tell he was a man's man. I noticed him quickly. He was popular at the job, and well liked. I had been kind of flirting with him, but I was told that he had a wife so that was as far as it went. Later, I found out that they were separated. On one of my days off, I saw him at Bank of America. Me and my sister were about to go shopping and I told her that was that guy I was talking about. I called him over to the car and introduced them. He had the nerve to tell me, "You shouldn't have taken my number if you wasn't going to use it." I didn't know who he thought he was talking to but I liked it. He had a pleasant demeanor about him and everybody had only good things to say about him. Travis was from Hollis Queens, NY.

So, I took his advice and we began talking on the phone, then went on a few dates and just continued to get to know each other. We kept our friendship low-key because there were some messy people at our job and we didn't want everybody in our business. I also had my guard up because I didn't want to rush into anything, but the chemistry was definitely there. But being that we had a lot in common, it brought us closer together very quickly. We started to connect on so many levels that I decided to give him a chance. After six months of dating, he decided to move in with me and my son. I had a two-bedroom apartment in a complex where my sister worked. She wasn't too happy when I moved out but the boys, her two sons and my son, were getting too big to share a room.

I also wanted to get my own place because I knew my brother was going to be coming home soon and I was sending him a one-way ticket to Georgia. Too much stuff was going on in New York and I thought the slower pace of the south would do him some good.

When my lease was up, Travis and I decided to move a few houses down to a townhouse, which had an upstairs and downstairs with three bathrooms and a porch in the back, instead of the front. I loved it from day one until someone broke into our house twice in a six-month time span. The first time, Tyheem got everything back. We found out that some kids did it and had most of the stuff on the property in a broken storage area. The second time, we never found out anything, so we moved. The detective handling the case was always too busy and even when I gave him the information, I was told that there wasn't much that they could do because they were minors. We stayed there until our lease was up, then we moved.

I finally connected with Glen and sent him the information for his ticket to his daughter Laquana. When he arrived, he started meeting people and adjusting to his surroundings. He was having a hard time finding steady work because of his background and he didn't have a vehicle so it was even harder. The plan was for him to stay with me for a while and if all else failed to try another state. I was so happy that we were all together. I knew my parents were smiling down on us, knowing that we still had each other's back.

In the meantime, Aliceia had been telling me about this guy who worked at the complex. He continued to tell her that she had the same last name as his aunt's husband. He went on to say that they also looked alike, talked alike and both were from New York, but he was from Queens. Every time they tried to meet up something happened. The more we talked about it, the more anxious I became. I spoke to my brother via letters and he was curious as well. Finally, they met up and my sister said when she got off the bus the resemblance was remarkable. I talked to him on the phone a couple of times and couldn't wait to meet him.

When I dropped Tyheem off that summer, he came to my sisters. He would come over on Fridays and leave on Sunday. He looked a lot like my Uncle Jimmy whose real name was James, but a little taller than my brother with the same complexion and smile and the same sense of humor like my father. My father's side of the family were Jehovah Witnesses, and my aunt got pregnant at an early age, so she gave up the child for adoption and disappeared. My father rarely ever talked about her or the child she gave up. Come to find out from my cousin, he was adopted and had inquired about any family members he may have had but received no luck. All of my father's brothers were deceased and we couldn't find his only sister.

I wished that we could have found him sooner, but nevertheless, I was thankful that we were together. Sometimes he reminded me of my father with his mouth. No filter, tall, and he kept it gully all the time. I loved him dearly. When I first saw him, I just kept smiling and couldn't wait for my brother to meet him as well. He told us a story about the cops stopping him one day in Queens stating that he fit the description of someone they were looking for. They were actually looking for my brother. We continued to spend time together because we believed tomorrow wasn't promised to anyone. I was so thankful to have him in my life.

When January rolled around, I decided to have two birthday parties, one on Friday and one on Sunday. On Saturday, Alecia invited me and Travis to an all-black affair that one of her coworkers was giving. Come to find out, the party on Saturday was a surprise engagement party for me. Travis got down on one knee and proposed. I was so happy and very emotional. I couldn't control my tears. In my heart, I knew this was different from any love I had experienced before. Travis was different. He had my back. He wasn't jealous. He could mingle with my family and friends and be there for me with ease. He even surprised me again and made sure my best friend, Sequana from New York, was there too.

It's funny because I was telling my sister that he had been acting funny lately and was possibly cheating on me. Come to find out, he was making plans for my friend's arrival, picking out rings and

CHAPTER 8

arranging the party to make sure that people got there before us.

I said yes, in between tears. My heart was beating so fast because I was totally taken by surprise and very excited that my sister and brother gave him their blessings. We made plans to get married the following May the week after Mother's Day. Planning a wedding was very stressful, and our main problem was finding a place big enough that was affordable. When we talked to people everybody had something to say, but not too many people were willing to assist or offer any money. We had a budget that I tried to stick to, but I couldn't. Even though I refused to go broke for one day, I wanted to have certain things such as real flowers, limousine service, a D.J. and a photographer. I wanted this wedding to be different from my first one.

My bridal party was awesome. My friend Takiyah allowed us to have the rehearsal at her house. Alohma sent us on our honeymoon to St. Croix, and my sister paid for part of my package for my pictures. Swans and Krissy did my invitations and Asia's husband played the music. Takiyah's brother, Ali, was the bartender and my coworkers helped serve the food. The wedding was beautiful. The only problem was the piece that was ordered for the air conditioner did not arrive so it started to get very hot and uncomfortable.

Instead of taking pictures at the venue, we took pictures at Centennial Park in downtown Atlanta. Everybody was taking pictures of us, and I felt like a princess in a fairytale. I had over twenty people in the bridal party and over 100 guests. We planned an after-party at one of the local bars not far from the center. I was so happy that my cousins Sherri, Vanessa, Lavasia and Tyrone were able to make it as well as my nieces Dakira, Deanna and Laquanna. Laquanna's husband, David, my nephew Glen Jr. and my great-nephews, Xavier and Messiah were there as well. One of the groomsmen, my co-worker Mr.

Pat, got sick but he continued to hang out with us the entire time. He even came to the after party at J.R. Crickets. A lot of our coworkers were very supportive as well. Even those who could not make it still gave us their blessings as well as gifts and gifts cards.

I've come to learn that there were a lot of people who said that they didn't believe in getting a divorce and 9 times out of 10 they were the same ones who had never been married. You never know what you're going to go through until you have that experience. I never judged people by the choices they made because if I hadn't walked a mile in their shoes. I didn't know what they were going through.

I continued to pray and ask God to give me a sign if I was making a mistake, not just in my marriage but in my everyday life challenges. As I went through life, and I reflected back on different situations, I noticed little things that were put in my way to warn me when danger was ahead, but most of the time, I either ignored it or did something against my better judgment.

Throughout the years, I have been truly blessed. I have been doing a lot of traveling. Growing up we didn't have money to take vacations. Yes, my father did bring us to Delaware a couple of times but I had never been on an airplane or had a desire to visit another country until I got older and started to educate myself. My first real vacation was in the early 90s. Some of my neighbors, the Taylors and John Webster Junior had all relocated to Pennsylvania and they invited us down for the weekend. We had a ball reconnecting, eating, drinking, playing double dutch, laughing, talking and catching up on each other's lives. My next vacation was to Montego Bay, Jamaica; Soon after I traveled to West Virginia, Virginia, St. Croix, St. Kitts, St. Marten, Florida, Ohio, Texas, Vegas, Puerto Rico, and New Orleans.

I also took Tyheem, as well as other family members and friends

CHAPTER 8

when I could. I thought it was important to learn about other cultures and how they lived. You couldn't believe everything you saw on television or on the internet.

Travis and I got along great and most importantly my son loved him. It was very important to me that he had a good relationship with him. Travis was very hard working and handy around the house. He could fix almost anything. We went out a lot to restaurants, clubs, comedy shows, took vacations, made road trips and attended church. We both enjoyed listening to music and dancing and he also liked to cook and was very good at it. He reminded me of my father.

Our toughest moment was having to discuss his children. I didn't want any baby mama drama. From the start, one of his children's mothers didn't want me around the kids, which was a little upsetting, but I dealt with it; as long as his relationship with the mother didn't affect our relationship, I was good.

I wasn't really planning on having any more children, but I said if I ever got married again and my husband wanted a child I would have one more. We had discussed it but two more unfortunate situations put a damper on that from happening. The first time I got pregnant it was only five months into the relationship. I really wasn't planning on keeping the child, but I had a lot of mixed feelings. We were just starting to get to know one another.

The second one occurred around six months later. I kept feeling really tired all the time but I thought it was because I was working so much then I missed my period. I took a home pregnancy test and it came out negative. The next month I started spotting but it was burgundy colored, which was unusual. The next day I didn't see anything so I got to work and different smells started to irritate me, making me feel nauseous and I began throwing up.

When I got home, I started cramping. I called my sister for some advice and she told me that I should go to the emergency room. At the time I didn't have health insurance so I decided to go to Grady Community Hospital. We sat there for about two hours and the smell of funk, blood and urine was in the air. People were laying all over the seats. They were mostly homeless people. I kept gagging and the pain was getting worse on my right side. Finally, my sister asked the receptionist how long the wait was, the receptionist gave a shitty response and my sister returned and said let's go. We went to a private hospital. I was reluctant because I knew that I would have to pay a huge bill, but the pain was increasing. The hospital was so much nicer, cleaner and they took me to the back within thirty to forty minutes. The nurses were friendly and it smelled good. I gave the triage nurse all of my information, and they took my weight, blood pressure, then drew some blood and took a urine sample. They had me dress down into a hospital gown open to the back and then sent me into the room for a sonogram. I told the nurse that I was cold and she gave me a blanket that was so warm I knew it just came out the dryer. The room was pretty small and dark. Travis helped me out the wheelchair and onto the bed. The doctor told me to lift my gown and she placed gel on my stomach, while looking at the monitor. She told me that I might be having another miscarriage and said if my numbers went up they would have to sew my cervix to ensure the safety of the fetus. They could possibly save the baby, however, she said if the numbers went down then there was nothing they could do.

I tried my best not to get too excited or tell too many people just in case I lost it again. I started talking to a few friends and family,

CHAPTER 8

trying to figure out my babysitting arrangement and time off from work.

We went over to my sister's house for a barbeque and everything tasted so good. I was eating up everything, but certain smells were bothering me and everything stunk. When we got home I started having some cramps. I thought maybe I ate too much and on the way home, my stomach started turning. I couldn't even make it to the bathroom upstairs so I used the one downstairs. When I sat down, I felt a sharp pain. I sat there for a while and I could feel a pulling sensation in my stomach. I got up and I saw a little blood in the toilet. I wiped myself and saw some mucous on the tissue. The pain started again. I pulled myself up to go upstairs, and I took a hot shower and went to bed.

The next day, when I used the restroom, I was still spotting a little. On the third day, I was using the restroom after work and I felt a gush and I saw little clots of blood falling into the toilet and yelled, "NO, NO, NO!"

Travis ran downstairs and said, "What's wrong?" I said, "The baby. I'm losing the baby." I sat there rocking back and forth, holding my stomach.

We rushed to the emergency room where I undressed, put on a gown and entered the room to take a sonogram. The nurse continued to roll the device over my stomach, snapping pictures. She said she was going to have to do a prenatal sonogram because the image was too small. She told me to slide all the way down and place my legs in the stirrups. Then she inserted the device that looked like a microphone into my vagina and began to take pictures. I was looking at the monitor and I didn't see anything. I looked at the nurse and she had a flat affect on her face. I asked, "Do you see it? Am I still pregnant?"

"I'm sorry." She apologized.

I just cried, tears rolling down my face. Travis rubbed my hand and told me that everything was going to be okay. The ride home was very quiet. I just held my stomach and fell asleep. When I got home, I took a shower and laid in the bed. I felt so empty inside. But that loss made Travis and I even closer.

The next year I lost a close family friend, a nephew and a cousin. Death was always so difficult to understand. You could be here today and gone tomorrow. This was one of the reasons I tried so hard to stay in touch with people and continued to keep some type of communication.

Now, in the year 2018, there's really no reason why you can't keep in touch with people. You can go the old-fashioned way and write them a letter, call them on the phone, send them a text message or even an email. No matter how near or far, continue to show people how much you care and let them know that you are thinking about them. People grow up, move on and relocate, but true friendship will always prevail.

My journey has been eventful. I've married my soulmate. My brother and sister and I are doing well, and there is so much love between us, our children, and the hundreds of other family members. I believe our parents would be proud. I know I am.

The end.

EPILOGUE

Over the years I've met quite a few people from New York who relocated to Atlanta. People have made this decision for different reasons and I'm glad that they are a part of my circle of friends. There are also a lot of stereotypes and misconceptions about either New York or Georgia and I hope their stories can help clarify some rumors and answer some of the often asked, questions.

According to my coworker and friend, Lucky, who resided in Queens, New York and Atlanta, Georgia, "I moved to Atlanta for a change of the environment because the streets were raising us. I got tired of seeing people get shot at by kids we grew up with, then expect you not to tell. People always getting killed over fashion such as sneakers and jewelry. There was not much to look forward to."

I used to hear people say that Atlanta was like a little New York. I totally disagree because according to the population of both places; metro Atlanta is estimated to be about 5.6 million people compared to New York City, whose estimate is 19.1 million people. The train system, New York City Transit Authority, rides are approximately one long hour from the first stop to the last stop. Atlanta Marta station runs from North to East and South to West. The commutes are much longer. Brooklyn alone is estimated at 2.6 million people. According to Travis Ward, "I relocated to Georgia to give my kids a better life. I've heard rumors that Georgia is like New York and I totally disagree. New York never sleeps but Georgia shuts down at 3am." I don't think I would ever move back to New York. First of all, the cost of living has gone up since I've been gone. For example, a two-bedroom apartment in New York is approximately $1700 a month compared to Atlanta, Georgia, which goes for approximately $800 a month. Full coverage car insurance on a vehicle in New York is approximately $400 a month compared to Atlanta, which is approximately $125 a month.

Relocating for me, was about creating a better, more affordable, living environment. What I miss about New York is the night life. Aliceia McCray stated, "I moved to Georgia because there were better opportunities for employment in my field which is property management. Georgia is much smaller than New York. When I moved to Georgia, I had never been there and did not know one single person. It was just me and my two sons, ages five and eight. I was running out of money and needed a job. My rent was taken care of, so I wasn't worried about that. I started working at an apartment management staffing agency on a temporary to permanent basis. I didn't want to raise my boys in New York because the gangs were becoming a big problem in my neighborhood and they were at the age where they wanted to go outside alone. I had fears of my sons being harassed by the police or possibly targeted because they hung out in groups.

In New York, there are a lot of parks. In Georgia, you might have to drive to a park to allow the kids to play. Most houses have the front and backyard but you have to worry about the kids running into traffic. Also, chances are you don't have a lot of things for the kids to do in your front or backyard and not too many other children their age.

I'm used to people speaking what's on their mind. People in Georgia will throw you under the bus then ask you what happened. New Yorkers keeps it real. Georgia is called the dirty south for a reason. I've made very few friends because of this. I'm always on point and live like I'm still in the big city. New York and Georgia are like apples and oranges. Oops I mean peaches."

www.ingramcontent.com/pod-product-compliance
Lightning Source LLC
Chambersburg PA
CBHW020426010526
44118CB00010B/445